Dramatic Programs for Christmas

268.7

Dramatic Programs for Christmas

Cecil McGee

BROADMAN PRESS
Nashville, Tennessee

3717

JEFFERSON AVENUE BAPTIST CHURCH LIBRARY

© Copyright 1970 • Broadman Press
All rights reserved

4275-07

All Scripture references
except where noted
are from the *King James Version.*
Dewey Decimal Classification Number: 268.7
Library of Congress Catalog Card Number: 74-93917
Printed in the United States of America
3.5My7018

CONTENTS

1. **Light of the World** (candlelight service) — 1
2. **Cradle to Cross** (Scripture, poetry, and spirituals) — 7
3. **Joseph, a Father to the King** (featuring a monologue) — 13
4. **And There Were Shepherds** (featuring a story) — 22
5. **A Stable Boy** (a story and slides) — 32
6. **The Miracle** (a contemporary play) — 39
7. **Tell It Again** (a storyteller in a contemporary setting) — 46
8. **Whose Birthday Is It, Anyway?** (puppet play) — 55
9. **White Christmas** (missions emphasis, featuring a story) — 65
10. **The Christmas Story** (speech choir, music, tableaux) — 82
11. **Christmas Eve Family Worship** (to be used in homes) — 87
12. **The Inn That Missed Its Chance** (a dialogue) — 90
13. **Jesus, the Savior** (featuring three monologues) — 94

How-to Instructions — 104

Index — 113

PREFACE

This book has been prepared with a deep desire that the purpose of Christ's coming might be magnified.

"And she shall bring forth a son, and thou shalt call his name JESUS: for he shall save his people from their sins."

What exciting good news from the angel of the Lord! What marvelous hope for a troubled, frustrated world!

The programs in this book take us to the manger and far beyond—to a cross—and to an empty tomb! A variety of dramatic techniques is used to present each message with animation and aliveness. Dramatic techniques need not be complicated to be effective. In fact, the simpler they are, the greater the impact.

Each program included is flexible and can easily be adapted to fit the needs of any group. Staging requirements are such that small churches will have no difficulty in presenting the programs.

Many variations will be possible in each program. Most churches will have special talent available that can be used. For example, a trumpet and other musical instruments will add excitement to any program.

CECIL MCGEE

Light of the World

The following candlelight feature is designed to conclude a Christmas time service. Establish an atmosphere of worship through the prelude, Christmas hymns, prayer, the offering, and Christmas music presented by the various age groups. Let each singing group come to the platform for its presentation and then return to seats in the congregation, leaving the platform and choir space free for the closing feature.

HYMN: "The Light of the World Is Jesus"
(*Have the first stanza sung by a choir, ensemble, or soloist from the back of the auditorium.*)

PASTOR OR LEADER: "And God said, Let there be light: and there was light. And God saw the light, that it was good: and God divided the light from the darkness."

A pillar of light guided the wandering feet of the children of Israel through the wilderness, and God has provided light for the journeyings of men ever since. When the prophet of old spoke of the coming Messiah, he used the language of light!

(*Repeat the chorus of "The Light of the World Is Jesus," during which time* ISAIAH *enters, carrying a large, burning candle. Houselights are dimmed out or turned off as* ISAIAH *approaches. When all overhead lights are out,* JOSEPH *and* MARY *slip into their tableau position for nativity scene, in the baptistry.*)

Isaiah: "The people that walked in darkness have seen a great light." (*Spotlight nativity scene.*) "For unto us a child is born, unto us a son is given: and the government shall be upon his shoulder: and his name shall be called Wonderful, Counsellor, The mighty God, The everlasting Father, The Prince of Peace.

"Of the increase of his government and peace there shall be no end, upon the throne of David, and upon his kingdom, to order it, and to establish it with judgment and with justice from henceforth even forever. The zeal of the Lord of hosts will perform this.

"Arise, shine; for thy light is come, and the glory of the Lord is risen upon thee."

(Isaiah *places his candle on a stand or small table that is elevated enough for all to see. He then exits during the following song.*)

Choir or Ensemble: "Angels, from the Realms of Glory" (*first stanza*).

(*After song, spot off of nativity. The organ continues playing and fades under the narrative.*)

Speech Choir (*speaking from the darkness*): "The people that walked in darkness have seen a great light."

(*The organ builds and continues playing as* Boy 1 *comes from the front row of the congregation and lights his candle from* Isaiah's *and then moves to the platform level for his Scripture reading. Five others will come up similarly. Use all possible levels in placing the six candlelighters. The organ fades under as* Boy 1 *speaks.*)

Boy 1: "The dayspring from on high hath visited us, to give light to them that sit in darkness."

Speech Choir: Light—to them that sit in darkness.
(*The organ music builds and continues as* Girl 1 *lights her*

candle and moves into place. *The organ fades under as* GIRL 1 *speaks.*)

GIRL 1: "For God, who commanded the light to shine out of darkness, hath shined in our hearts."

SPEECH CHOIR: God commanded the light to shine out of darkness.
(*The organ music builds as* BOY 2 *goes to light his candle and fades under when he is in his place.*)

BOY 2: "Jesus said, I am the Light of the world: he that followeth me shall not walk in darkness, but shall have the light of life."

SPEECH CHOIR: The light of life—(*softer*) The light of life—(*softer*) The light of life.
(*The music builds as* GIRL 2 *goes to light her candle.*)

GIRL 2: "God is light, and in him is no darkness at all."

SPEECH CHOIR: In him—no darkness! In him—no darkness at all!
(*The organ music builds as* BOY 3 *lights his candle and fades under as he speaks.*)

BOY 3: "The Lord is my light and my salvation; whom shall I fear?"

SPEECH CHOIR (*begin softly and build on each phrase*):
My light and my salvation.
My light and my salvation.
My light and my salvation.
WHOM SHALL I FEAR?

(*The organ music builds as* GIRL 3 *lights her candle.*)

GIRL 3: Jesus said, "Ye are the light of the world. Let your light so shine before men, that they may see your good works, and glorify your Father which is in heaven." "Arise, shine; for thy light is come!"

(*The singing groups that have sung earlier in the service sing "The Light of the World Is Jesus," or some other appropriate music, as they move to light their candles from the seven that are burning. After they light their candles, they take positions at the front and around the wall encircling the congregation. When all are in place and the music has been completed, the* PASTOR OR LEADER *speaks.*)

PASTOR OR LEADER: Christians are candles—candles by which the dark world is to be illuminated! A candle must be lighted from another's torch. The flame by which we burn is Christ. (*Spotlight nativity.*) There is for Christians no other source of light.

"Ye are the light of the world. Let your light so shine before men, that they may see your good works, and glorify your Father which is in heaven."

One candle may not shed much light, but many candles will brighten even the darkest place!

Those of you in the congregation who wish to do so may take a candle from the rack in front of you. If you are next to an aisle, light it from the burning candle nearest you, and return to your place. Share your light with the one next to you. This is an opportunity for each of us to silently express to God what we feel deep down in our heart. I invite you to join me in doing so right now.

(*The organ plays softly until all have had a chance to light their candles.*)

PASTOR OR LEADER: Our dark world needs desperately what you can give it. Will you share the light?

(*The* PASTOR OR LEADER *leads in a time of commitment. Before the benediction, he suggests that those who wish to do so may take their candles home with them. If it is put in a prominent place, it can serve during the holidays as a constant reminder of him whose birth we celebrate, Christ—the Light of the World! With candles still burning, ask the congregation to sing "Silent Night, Holy Night" as they leave.*)

Instructions for Candlelight Service

Platform Arrangement

The pastor should work from the floor level, leaving the platform free for the candlelighters.

In positioning the candlelighters, work for a pleasing picture in which all six can be clearly seen. Use the platform, the steps leading up to the platform, and any other possible levels.

Isaiah

Choose a man with a deep, rich voice. Challenge him to memorize the brief Scripture passages. Only then can he live them and meaningfully share them with the audience.

Costuming and Make-up

Isaiah, Joseph, and Mary will need biblical costumes. Beards will be needed for Isaiah and Joseph.

"How-to instructions" for making the beard and costume can be found at the end of the book.

Speech Choir

The speech choir is heard but not seen. They can be seated at the front of the auditorium, at the very back, or in a balcony.

See "How-to Instructions" for the speech choir.

Organ Music

Choose music that the organist can play without the use of light. Total darkness will heighten the effectiveness of the candlelight.

The Nativity

A sturdy table can be used to elevate the tableau in the baptistry. Light the scene from within the baptistry and be sure that the light source cannot be seen by the audience.

If the baptistry is not suitable for the scene, use the choir loft. Arrange the tableau as far away from the candlelighters as possible and elevate it so that it can be seen above the heads of the candlelighters.

In the final portion of the service, the characters in the tableau will need to remain in place, motionless, until the entire congregation has gone.

See "How-to Instructions" for arranging a tableau.

Candles

Isaiah's candle should be at least twelve inches tall and much larger in diameter than the other candles. Be sure to practice with the candle and candle holder so that there's no chance of it toppling over.

For the six candlelighters, use ten-inch tapers. Six-inch candles can be used by the congregation.

To keep the candles from dripping on hands and carpets, use a circle of white cardboard, about four inches in diameter. Punch a small hole in the center of the cardboard. Enlarge it until the small end of the candle will barely go through. Gently force the candle on up through the hole. Leave about half of it beneath the cardboard for a handle.

A slightly larger circle of cardboard will be needed for the ten-inch tapers. Do some experimenting.

Provide containers in the vestibule so that candles can be placed in them as people leave the service.

Cradle to Cross

In this program, Scripture, poetry, and spirituals are combined to present the birth, crucifixion, and resurrection of Jesus.

(Make this order of service different. After a prelude of Christmas carols, present the necessary announcements. Then set an atmosphere of worship with a congregational hymn and the offering. Let the rest of the program move along without any interruptions.)

PROCESSIONAL: "Go Tell It on the Mountain"
   (The choirs and other singing groups enter singing.)

CALL TO PRAYER: "Standing in the Need of Prayer"
   (Sung by a choir or small singing group, unaccompanied.)

PRAYER: *(Repeat the chorus during a moment of silent prayer. The pastor then leads in a brief, audible prayer. Turn off overhead lights during the prayer.)*

SPOTLIGHT: *Upon* READER *at the close of the prayer.*

READER: The birth of Jesus—The prophets foretold his coming.
   (From the darkness will come Scriptures done by two reading groups. Place one group in the very back of the auditorium and the other one in a balcony or at the front of the auditorium.)

GROUP 1: "Behold, a virgin shall be with child, and shall bring forth a son,

GROUP 2: And they shall call his name Emmanuel,

GROUP 1: Which being interpreted is, God with us.

GROUP 2: For unto us a child is born,

GROUP 1: Unto us a son is given:

GROUP 2: And the government shall be upon his shoulder:

GROUP 1: And his name shall be called *Wonderful,*

GROUP 2: *Counsellor,*

GROUP 1: *The mighty God,*

GROUP 2: *The everlasting Father,*

GROUP 1: *The Prince of Peace."*

READER: The birth of Jesus—angels foretold his coming.

GROUP 2: "And in the sixth month the angel Gabriel was sent from God

GROUP 1: Unto a city of Galilee, named Nazareth, to a virgin espoused to a man whose name was Joseph, of the house of David:

GROUP 2: And the virgin's name was Mary. And the angel came in unto her, and said,

ONE MALE VOICE: Hail, thou that art highly favoured, the Lord is with thee: blessed art thou among women.

GROUP 1: And when she saw him, she was troubled at his saying, . . . And the angel said unto her,

MALE VOICE: Fear not, Mary: for thou hast found favour with God. And, behold, thou shalt conceive in thy womb, and bring forth a son, and shalt call his name Jesus. He shall be great, and shall be called *the Son of the Highest.* . . .

GROUP 2: Then said Mary unto the angel,

FEMALE VOICES OF GROUP 1: How shall this be, seeing I know not a man?

GROUP 2: And the angel answered and said unto her,

MALE VOICE: The Holy Ghost shall come upon thee, and the power of the Highest shall overshadow thee: therefore also that holy thing which shall be born of thee shall be called the Son of God. . . . For with God nothing shall be impossible.

GROUP 1: And Mary said,

FEMALE VOICE: Behold, the handmaid of the Lord; be it unto me according to thy word."

READER: "And so it was, that, while they were there, the days were accomplished that she should be delivered. And she brought forth her firstborn son, and wrapped him in swaddling clothes, and laid him in a manger; because there was no room for them in the inn."

(JOSEPH *and* MARY *slip into place for the Nativity scene during the last Scripture.*)

SPOTLIGHT: *Off the* READER *and upon the Nativity.*

SOLOIST: "Sweet Little Jesus Boy"
(SOLOIST *is not seen.*)

READER (*From the darkness while attention is still focused on Nativity*):

SPOTLIGHT: *blue light on Nativity.*
"He is despised and rejected of men; a man of sorrows, and acquainted with grief. . . . He was wounded for our transgressions, he was bruised for our iniquities: the chastisement of our peace was upon him; and with his stripes we are healed."

SPOTLIGHT: *Off the Nativity and upon soloist.*

SOLOIST: "Jesus Walked This Lonesome Valley"
(*Use the* CHOIR, *unseen, as background for the soloist.*)

SPOTLIGHT: *Off the* SOLOIST *and upon Nativity with red light during the last chorus of the song.*
(*The* PERSON *who does the poem, "The Crucifixion," moves to his place in the darkness.*)

SPOTLIGHT: *Off the Nativity and upon the* POETRY READER *at the close of the solo.*

POETRY: "The Crucifixion," by James Weldon Johnson

SPOTLIGHT: *Off the reader and upon the Cross.*

CHOIR: "Were You There?"
(*Use the following stanzas:*)

> Were you there when they crucified my Lord?
> Were you there when they nailed him to the tree?
> Were you there when they laid him in the tomb?
> Were you there when he rose up from the grave?

SPOTLIGHT: *Off the Cross at the end of stanza 3. Flood the baptistry with the brightest lights possible for the singing of stanza 4.*

CHOIR: "Let Us Break Bread Together"
(*Let the* CHOIR *sing unaccompanied, unseen, with no light except that in the baptistry.*)

SILENT LORD'S SUPPER: (*As the choir sings, the pastor and deacons silently lead in the observance of the Lord's Supper. No words need be spoken.*)

SONG OF COMMITMENT: "Lord, I Want to Be a Christian"
(*Sung by choir and congregation, unannounced. Use the following stanzas:*)

> Lord, I want to be a Christian
> Lord, I want to be more loving

> Lord, I want to be more holy
> Lord, I want to be like Jesus

BENEDICTION

STAGING DIRECTIONS

Platform Arrangement

Seat the choir and other singing groups in the auditorium, rather than the choir loft. They will sing from where they're seated, unseen by the audience.

Let the reader work from the auditorium floor level in front of the pulpit area. Put his script in a black folder made of construction paper. He can sit on the front row when he is not speaking.

Elevate the Nativity so that it can be easily seen. Use sturdy tables for levels if the platform is not high enough.

The poetry reader should work from the platform level, as far away from the Nativity area as possible.

Use a crude, unpainted wooden cross eight to ten feet tall. Construct it so that it can easily be stood up and put in place in the darkness just before it is seen. Place it on the top level of the choir loft as far from the baptistry opening as possible. Be sure that it can be seen from all angles in the auditorium.

The Lord's Supper table will need to be already prepared and in place.

The Readers

Much of the success of this program depends on the readers. Choose the best ones available. Get them together at least six weeks in advance of the presentation. Put scripts in their hands and communicate to them the importance of what they are to do. Challenge them to make their reading a fresh, exciting experience for the audience.

The small reading groups will need to rehearse together several hours. See "How-to Instructions" for helping a speech choir.

The other two readers should also see the "How-to Instructions."

Source of Poetry

The poem, "The Crucifixion," by James Weldon Johnson comes from the book, *God's Trombones* by the same author, The Viking

Press, New York, New York. The book can be found in most city and school libraries and is available in book stores.

Source of Music

"Sweet Little Jesus Boy," words and music by Robert Mac Gimsey, Carl Fischer, Inc., New York, N.Y., available in music stores. (Medium Voice in F Major, Low Voice in D Major.) Recorded by Robert Merrill, RCA Victor, No. 10–1303.

The Nativity

"How-to Instructions" Offers help in creating tableaux.

Costuming, Make-up, Lighting, Scenery

See "How-to Instructions."

Rehearsals

Most of the rehearsing can be done with small groups and individuals. Be sure to schedule at least two full rehearsals with everybody who is to participate. Include costumes, make-up, sound, lights, and music. The pastor and others who serve the Lord's Supper should be included in the final rehearsal.

Joseph, a Father to the King

In this imaginative script, the events surrounding the birth of Jesus are beautifully told by Joseph and a narrator.

NARRATOR: Christianity—Christmas—in ultimates these are inseparable. When thinking of the origin of Christianity, our minds conjure up a traditional scene—a stable—a crib—a baby . . . Yes, this is where it began, in a city called Bethlehem, in a land called Judah. . . .

Though in the Divine Will and Wisdom, it could have just as well begun in a humble Oklahoma farm house plagued by dust and depression. . . .

Or for that matter it could have begun in the sterile delivery room of an ultramodern, scientifically equipped city hospital. For it is more than a *place* and a *time* that has made Christianity.

The story of Christianity's beginning—the Story of Christmas—has been told many times, in many ways, by many people. Yet, there is one who could tell it as none other has. For he knew it as no other man could.

His name?

His name was Joseph. Our Joseph was a man of wood and nails, a carpenter by trade. Joseph's name, along with his family lineage, placed him in the ancestral line of the great Hebrew King David. However, there was little about his humble home in Nazareth that would suggest he knew anything of a royal life.

And yet, how much closer can one come to true royalty than to be known as a Father to the King? But wait, let us pull back the shroud of the past, and let Joseph share with us how he, a man of common work and common ways, became the most honored of all men.

As I said, it all began in Bethlehem. Bethlehem, the city of Joseph's ancestors, was also the place of his birth. . . .

JOSEPH: Bethlehem? You ask of Bethlehem? Yes, I remember Bethlehem. Bethlehem had never been to me, the least among the Princes of Judah.

There was always a disturbing enchantment about Bethlehem. As a boy I often roamed the hills that encircled the city's humble walls. How I loved the hills of Bethlehem! As I lay upon the grassy slopes of the shepherd's pastures, reciting the lessons from the prophets, it seemed as if the listening hills whispered soft Amens in my ears. The narrow, crowded streets of Bethlehem hummed with the stories of Israel's past and the dreams of her future.

I was a youth blessed with devoutly pious parents, who saw to my instruction in the rich traditions and prophecies given to our fathers by the mighty Jehovah. Jacob's words were by no measure a match for his skilled hands, but his consistency in seeing to my daily study of the Scriptures, was equal to his sure striking mallet.

Jacob was by nature a gentle man, but it was a forceful hand that held mine that day we passed through Bethlehem's main gate. I thought surely my young heart would break as I saw the walls of my beloved city grow smaller and smaller in the distance. Our family was moving from Bethlehem to Nazareth. Bethlehem had been our home and our heritage. But the more recently settled Nazareth offered much work for a family of our trade. And so it was, that the family of Jacob, of Bethlehem, came to live in Nazareth.

Nazareth had no heritage, nor honor. But to me, Nazareth

proved to be a most blessed place. For it was in Nazareth that I met Mary.

Mary—small of stature, slight and slender: her dark brown Galilean eyes shone with a warm and comforting glow. Her olive skin as free from blemish as a temple lamb. Her voice—the voice of a deep and pure mountain stream. She moved with the poise and grace of a lovely cedar swaying in the breezes of Lebanon. To me, Mary was Israel in full bloom!

I was much older than Mary, and clearly a man of no great wealth. Mary was also from a humble home. But, I had given no thought to the matter of a dowry. Yet, I was never richer than the day Mary joined me in the pledge of Betrothal. Betrothal, according to our law, was a family pledge that sealed our union as husband and wife. Though at that time we had not observed the marriage ceremony, nor come to live together, our pledge could be broken only by a divorce.

It was at this time that I faced the most difficult and trying moments of my life. Never before had I faced such a testing of my faith in Jehovah—of my trust in Mary. I could never believe Mary unfaithful. Never! Such a thing was unthinkable—impossible! And yet—what other answer could there be? Mary was with child! A million words seemed to dash about in my heart that evening as Mary told me, though none of them seemed able to find their way to my lips. I could not speak. In that silent moment I looked deep into Mary's eyes. And as I did the candle's flickering light found reflection in the tears as they slipped silently down her cheeks. What I saw in Mary's eyes only added to my confusion. For her eyes spoke of no wrong, no shame, no guilt. Her eyes were the eyes of purity, of innocence, of love!

"This must have much thought, much prayer," I said to myself as I left Mary's home that night. Josiah, Mary's father, was right. This must be a quiet matter. I could not put Mary to the public mockery and shame prescribed by our customs.

It was while I was thinking further upon this matter that it happened. The sunrise had passed and turned into another sunset. I lay upon my bed only to toss for hours, as I had done the night before. Finally, the weight of the long waking hours closed my eyes. It was a strange sleep that followed—a sleep that proved to be more conscious than not. For when I awoke suddenly, in the mid of night, I awoke with that abrupt, complete clearness of mind that revealed I had been awake long before my eyes had agreed to open. I could not explain it, but there was no doubt in my mind—I believed his words! An angel came to me in a dream—a dream that was more real than life itself. He said to me, "Joseph, descendant of David, do not be afraid to take Mary as your wife. For that which is conceived in her is by the power of the Holy God. . . ."

NARRATOR: We can surely understand the fearful amazement that came over Joseph that night as the angel told him that the child Mary was to birth would be called Jesus—the one who delivers—and that he would save his people from their sins.

Joseph was beside himself with joy at the angelic message. The hour was late, but in Joseph's mind this matter would not be delayed til morning.

Arousing Josiah from his bed, and summoning Mary to his side, he told her of the angel's words. It was at this time that Mary told Joseph of an angel who had also come to her with greetings from Jehovah, calling her blessed, and saying that she had been chosen to bear a child—a Son. A Son who would be called the Son of God.

Now the time of Mary's fulfilment was drawing near and the long journey was not to Joseph's liking. But it was the time of the great enrolment. Thus, in keeping with Herod's decree calling for every father's son to return to the place of his birth to register for the taxation, Joseph took Mary and retraced his youthful steps back to the place of his birth—back to Bethlehem.

The way from Nazareth to Bethlehem was long, and due to Mary's condition it was slow. However, Joseph and Mary had arrived in Bethlehem well within the time set for the enrolment. The blessed city was filled with its sons who had come from near and far.

To Joseph, Bethlehem had never been an unkind place. "There was no real unkindness meant by her closed doors," Joseph assured Mary as they made their way through the multitudes in the streets. There were so many people, there was simply no room. No room for a peasant carpenter and his wife. No room—for the birth of a King!

Joseph and Mary had gone from door to door all day. The keepers of the city walls had already called out the announcement of the closing of the city gates. Night, like a mother hen hovering over her brood, was beginning to cover the city with its dark wings. The air seemed to speak a chilled warning of coming discomfort. It was in near despair that Joseph faced Kaleb's Inn. It was one of the few doors in the entire city at which he had not already knocked that day. Joseph paused for a moment, he looked to the Inn—then to Mary—

JOSEPH: "It is a humble place," I said to Mary, "perhaps here"—
The man spoke with kindness, but as he shrugged his shoulders in a motion of finality, it seemed as if there were no room in the world for Mary and her child. As I turned to leave, the woman who had been standing behind the innkeeper cried out, "Wait."

She whispered in her husband's ear.

He looked at Mary, then he nodded agreeing with his wife, and said, "My friend, we have no room, but there is a stable. It is growing late and your wife is tired. If you wish, you are welcome to spend the night there."

It was "humble quarters," but as the silent hands of the night took hold of Bethlehem, it was a welcomed place. It was only a stable, but that night it became for a moment a palace—a temple—the very nursery of heaven.

The innkeeper's wife had done her best to make the stable warm and comfortable for Mary. And as if summoned by the calls of my heart, she suddenly reappeared in the doorway of the stable a few hours later. She did not speak as she stood there in the doorway looking at Mary. She smiled, and without a word busied herself about the task of helping Mary.

The time of Mary's fulfilment had come. The long awaited moment was here at last—the child was being born!

I stepped outside the stable for a moment. I had not noticed it before, but the heavens seemed unusually bright. And right above the stable, high in the sky, there was a star like I had never seen. Its light shone in the heavens like a torch, like a celestial signal sending its mysterious message of light in every direction. I stood there transfixed by its light. The only sounds to be heard were the silent sounds of Bethlehem that seemed to be calling out to me from my youth. They were the sounds of inaudible music that choruses in one's heart as he beholds the simple beauty of earth, and sky and star. It was then that I heard a cry. The cry of a baby. It was no different from the cry of many infants I had heard in Nazareth. And yet, it was a cry that seemed to be the signal for the whole world to bow in awe, and praise, and prayer.

How did I feel? What were my thoughts as I looked upon that child? I could never fully tell you; no not in a thousand lifetimes. How does one tell what it is like to behold the birth of a King?

As I looked, I looked with eyes filled with wonder and worship. My mind was flooded with all the promises of the prophets I had known from my youth—with the strange visions and messages of the angels in Nazareth. But what was the meaning of this? How could it be? How could even God accomplish so much with so little? Did I dare hope, dare dream, dare believe? Did I dare believe that this infant, whose first glimpse of glory was the walls of a simple stable, was in fact the son of the Almighty God? Did I dare believe that in him God was coming among us—did I dare believe? . . . Did I dare?

Though we had told no one of the child's birth, it seemed as if the whole world had received announcement of his arrival. Shepherds, who had left their flocks in the fields, came filled with joy and excitement asking of a child; a child they said, angels had told them was born in Bethlehem. Their stammering lips were laden with a strange song they claimed a heavenly host had given them—a song of peace, of good will, of glory to God.

My heart was filled with feelings, convictions that I could not explain nor express. And yet, as I looked at the shepherds bowing in praise before the child; and later, as I witnessed the Wise Men who had followed the star to Bethlehem, bowing humbly to encircle the child with their precious gifts, I knew. Somehow I knew. I did not fully understand it but—deep within I knew.

There were many times after that when I was bewildered and confused over that night and its meaning. There was the day of the purification. Mary and I had taken the child up to Jerusalem to offer a sacrifice in keeping with the law. As we entered the temple, a priest, seeing the child in Mary's arms, announced, "Now my eyes have seen the salvation of the Lord. . . ."

There was also that day at the temple, some twelve years later, when Jesus disturbed the rulers by his understanding of the Scriptures. But, really these are but a few of many such days. For this curly-headed youth, known as the carpenter's son, was destined to disturb the hearts and minds of all who came to know him!

Oh, I do not mean to say that Jesus was ever anything

less than a boy. He loved hills, and sky and stream. His heart, as the heart of any youth, ran with the wind in the fields. His ears loved the sounds of nature. His voice bespoke the hopes and dreams of true youth. But—if he was never anything less than a boy, he was likewise never anything less than the Son of the Living God—in him, God had come among us—God among us.

NARRATOR: As the silence of history might suggest, death called upon Joseph while Jesus was still a very young man. It was during one of Galilee's severe winters. Joseph's health had begun to fail over the past few years and the chill of that winter seemed too much for him to endure. And so it was, that while death stood at his door like a patient friend, awaiting his moment of departure, Joseph called his family to his side. Kissing each and reminding them of their responsibility to the law of their fathers, Joseph said his farewells.

As Joseph looked upon Jesus that night—now tall in stature, strong of arm, and gentle of nature—it seemed for a moment that he stood once again in another place, at another time.

Joseph had thought of Bethlehem, of that night many times over the years—many times. He had never beheld the sight of a simple star in the heavens that he had not remembered that night a child was born to a carpenter's wife—that night when by Heaven's gift he had become for a moment a father to the King! Suddenly his mind was filled once again with the music of angels—with the scenes of a stable, of shepherds, of Wise Men—of a baby!

Yes, in those last moments, as on that night long ago in Bethlehem, Joseph knew it was so—

His heart echoed the words of the prophet: "The Lord himself shall give you a sign; Behold a Virgin shall conceive and bear a son, and shall call his name Immanuel— GOD AMONG US!!"

Yes, unto us, a child was born—unto us God's Son was given!

His name?

His name was Joseph—carpenter of Nazareth, husband to Mary, ah, but for a moment—a father to THE KING!

STAGING DIRECTIONS

"Joseph—A Father to the King" can be presented by one actor or two.

One Actor

When one actor plays the role of JOSEPH and the NARRATOR, the dress should be a light colored business suit and a long dark stole. When speaking as JOSEPH, the stole is draped from one shoulder across the front of the speaker. When the NARRATOR speaks, the stole is dropped to the floor and held in one hand. Each part should be spoken from a prearranged and appropriately lighted spot on the stage. JOSEPH should be played from a more up-stage spot. The NARRATOR played down stage and somewhat to the side of JOSEPH's spot. The NARRATOR should not block the audience's view of JOSEPH's spot. The transition from one character to the other should not be hurried but distinct.

Two Actors

When a separate actor is used to portray both JOSEPH and the NARRATOR, the above notes regarding locations of actors should be employed. Controlled lighting can be an added factor. Dimming the lights that are on the character not speaking will add good effects. The matter of dress may also be an added feature. The NARRATOR should dress in a business suit. JOSEPH should be dressed in appropriate biblical costuming. The flow of speech from one actor to the other should be smooth and unhurried.

And There Were Shepherds

In this program, the story of Jesus' birth is told by one of the shepherds. The program involves two readers, a storyteller, several singing groups, and a tableau.

(*Begin the service by singing some of the best-loved carols. Make necessary announcements. Establish an atmosphere for the rest of the program by singing, "While Shepherds Watched Their Flocks." Take the offering, unannounced, at the close of the song. Let the prayer come at the close of the offering. Dim the overhead lights or turn most of them off during the offertory prayer.*)

PROCESSIONAL: CANDLELIGHTERS *enter down the aisles, singing, "O Holy Night," in unison, unaccompanied.* (*Use six to eight junior high or senior high girls. Turn off all overhead lights as they enter.*) *As they sing, they light candles in the windows and at the front of the church. When all the candles are lighted, the* CHOIR *enters singing the second stanza and chorus. Seat the* CHOIR *in the auditorium rather than in the choir loft.*

(READERS 1 AND 2 *are stationed in the very back of the auditorium or in a balcony and read without being seen. Use a boy and a girl or a man and a woman.*)

READER 1 (male): "And there were in the same country shepherds abiding in the field,

READER 2: Keeping watch over their flock by night. And, lo, the angel of the Lord came upon them,

BOTH READERS: and the glory of the Lord shone round about them: and they were sore afraid.

READER 2: And the angel said unto them,

READER 1: Fear not: for, behold, I bring you good tidings of great joy, which shall be to all people. For unto you is born this day in the city of David a Saviour, which is Christ the Lord. And this shall be a sign unto you; ye shall find the babe wrapped in swaddling clothes, lying in a manger.

READER 2: And suddenly there was with the angel a multitude of the heavenly host praising God, and saying,

READER 1: Glory to God in the highest, and on earth peace, good will toward men.

READER 2: And it came to pass, as the angels were gone away from them into heaven, the shepherds said one to another,

BOTH READERS: Let us now go even unto Bethlehem, and see this thing which is come to pass, which the Lord hath made known unto us."

(*Five or more* SHEPHERDS *enter singing, "While by My Sheep," found on page 24. They move to the platform and group themselves informally, some sitting, some kneeling, and some standing. Station the echo choir as far away from the shepherds as possible and where they cannot be seen.*)

SHEPHERDS: *"While by My Sheep"*

(*They exit as they sing the last stanza, going in the opposite direction from which they came. As the sounds from the echo choir fade away, two other shepherds appear. One is an old man and the other his twelve-year-old grandson. They talk as they enter and move to the platform. See "The Shepherd's Story" on page 26 for their dialogue.*)

While by My Sheep

Old German
English Version by Theodore Baker, alt.

17th Century German Carol
Arranged by Hugo Jungst
Ed. by William J. Reynolds

1. While by my sheep I watched at night Glad tidings brought an angel bright:
2. There shall be born, so he did say, In Bethlehem a child to day:
3. There shall he lie, in manger mean, Who shall redeem the world from sin:
4. Lord, ever more to me be nigh, Then shall my heart be filled with joy:

How great my joy! Great my joy! Joy, joy, joy! Joy, joy, joy! Praise we the Lord on high with joy! Praise we the Lord on high with joy!

© Copyright 1970, Broadman Press. All rights reserved. International copyright secured.

DIALOGUE: "The Shepherd's Story"

(*Attention is focused on the dialogue scene until the close of the following line in the story*: "We hastened to the mouth of the cave; and there beheld our King." *Spotlight the Nativity scene with* MARY, JOSEPH, *and the* SHEPHERDS. *Let the dialogue continue in the darkness. Bring the spotlight back upon the dialogue scene for the last sentence:* "In the early morning we came back again to stand again in the place where the glory of God had shone and the music of heaven had filled the air."

As the OLD MAN *and* BOY *exit, repeat stanza one of the song,* "While by My Sheep." *This time, both singing groups are unseen.*)

PASTOR OR LEADER: How fitting it was that lowly shepherds were the first men to see and worship Jesus, the child later generations would call the Good Shepherd. Isaiah said:
"He shall feed his flock like a shepherd: he shall gather the lambs with his arm, and carry them in his bosom, and shall gently lead those that are with young."

The eastern shepherds led their sheep, they did not drive them. Each ram, ewe, and lamb had a name and when the shepherd called, the sheep came to his side.

The job of the shepherd was one of hardship and danger. He was exposed to the extremes of heat and cold, food was scanty, and he was ever subject to attack by wild animals.

Sheep are mentioned in the Bible about five hundred times. The people of God are his sheep.

Jesus said, "I am the good shepherd, and know my sheep, and am known of mine. I lay down my life for the sheep."

What a beautiful picture of the Christian's relationship to Christ is painted in the Shepherd Psalm!

(*Lead the congregation in quoting Psalm 23. You read a phrase and have them echo it. Close the service with a time of commitment and prayer.*)

Staging Directions

Candlelighters

Rehearse enough times that the lighting of the candles can be perfectly timed with the singing. To avoid candle drippings, see "How-to Instructions."

Tableau

"How-to Instructions" give helps for forming tableaux.

The Story

"The Shepherd's Story" can be done by one person, a storyteller, dressed in contemporary clothing.

Work to make the reading of God's Word exciting. Be sure every word can be heard and understood. See "How-to Instructions" for creative reading.

Costuming, Make-up, Lighting, Scenery

For information see "How-to Instructions."

Music

The song, "O Holy Night" can be found in the *Broadman Hymnal*, Broadman Press, 127 Ninth Avenue North, Nashville, Tennessee. The book is available in Baptist Book Stores.

The Shepherd's Story
Washington Gladden

"Bring hither that sheepskin, Joseph, and lay it down on this bank of dry earth, under this shelving rock. The wind blows chilly from the west, but the rock will shelter us. The sky is fair and the moon is rising, and we can sit here and watch the flocks on the hillside below. Your young blood and your father's coat of skins will keep you warm for one watch, I am sure. At midnight, my son, your father, Reuben, and his brother James will take our places; for the first watch the old man and the boy will tend the sheep."

"Yes, grandfather; you shall sit in that snug corner of the rock, where you can lean back and take your comfort. I will lie here at your feet. Now and then I will run to see whether the sheep are wandering, and that will warm me, if I grow cold."

"Have you never been out on the hills at night with your father?"

"Never, grandfather. I have often begged him to let me come; but he kept saying that I must wait until I was twelve years old. On the last full moon was my birthday and today, when he returned from Bethlehem to the flocks, he brought me with him."

"So this is the lad's first night with the sheep in the fields, and the old man's last night, I fear," said the aged shepherd, sadly. "It is not often in these days that I venture out to keep the watches of the flock; but this one night of the year I have spent upon these hills these many years, and I always shall as long as I have strength to walk so far."

"Was your father, too, a shepherd?"

"Yes, and all his fathers before him for many generations. On these hills my ancestors have kept their sheep for I know not how long.

"Do you not know, my boy, that this is the night of the year on which the Lord Christ was born?"

"Oh! yes," answered the lad. "My father told me as we were walking hither today, but I had forgotten it. And you were with the sheep that night?"

"Aye."

"Where was it?"

"Here, on this very spot."

The boy's eyes began to grow and fill with wonder and there was a slight tremor in his voice as he hurriedly plied the aged man with his eager questions. Stephanus drew his shepherd's cloak around him, and leaned forward a little, and looked out upon the silent moonlit hills, and then up into the sky.

"How long ago was that, grandfather?"

"Just fifty years ago this night."

"And how old were you then?"

"Fourteen, and a stout boy for my age. I had been for two

years in the fields with my father, and had tasted to the full the hardships and dangers of the shepherd's life."

"Who were you with on that night?"

"My father, and his brother, James, and Hosea, the son of John, a neighbor and kinsman of ours. That night, when the sun went down and the stars came out we were sitting here, upon this hillside, talking of the troubles of Israel and of the promises of deliverance spoken by the prophets; and James and Hosea were asking my father questions, and he was answering them, for he was older than they, and all the people of Bethlehem reverenced him as a wise and devout man.

"Suddenly I saw my father rise to his feet. Then the other men sprang up, with astonishment and wonder upon their faces. It had grown light all at once, lighter than the brightest moon; and as I turned my face in the direction in which the others were looking I saw, standing there upon that level place, a figure majestic and beautiful beyond all the power of words to tell."

"Were you not afraid, grandfather?"

"Indeed I was, my boy. My heart stopped beating. The others were standing, but I had no power to rise. I lay there motionless upon the earth. My eyes were fixed upon that wonderful face; upon those clear, shining eyes; upon that brow that seemed to beam with the purity of the soul within. It was not a smile with which that face was lighted. It was something too noble and exalted to call by that name. It was a look that told of power and peace, of joy and triumph."

"Did you know that it was an angel?"

"I knew not anything. I only knew that what I saw was glorious, too glorious for mortal eyes to look upon. And when he spoke, his voice, clearer than any trumpet and sweeter than any lute, charmed away all my fears.

"'Be not afraid' he said, 'for behold I bring you good tidings of great joy which shall be to all people. For there is born to you this day, in the City of David, a Saviour, which is Messiah, the King. And this is the sign unto you. Ye shall find a babe wrapped in swaddling clothes and lying in a manger.'

"And then, before we had time to make reply, he turned aside a little and lifted his face toward heaven, and, in a tone far louder than that in which he had spoken to us, but yet so sweet that it did not startle us at all, came forth from his lips the first strain of the great song:

"'Glory to God in the highest!'

"When he had uttered that, he paused a moment, and the echoes, one after another, from the hills that were near and hills that were far away, came flying home to us; so that I knew for once what the prophet meant when he said that all the mountains and the hills should break forth into singing. But before the echoes had all faded we began to hear other voices above our heads, a great chorus, taking up the strain that the angel first had sung. At first it seemed dim and far away; but gradually it came nearer, and filled the air, filled all the earth, filled all our souls with a most entrancing sweetness. Glory to God in the highest!—that was the grandest part. It seemed as though there could be no place so high that that strain would not mount up to it, and no place so happy that that voice would not make it thrill with new gladness. But then came the softer tones, less grand, but even sweeter: 'Peace on earth; good will to men.'"

"Did you see the choir of angels overhead, grandfather?"

"Nay, I saw nothing. The brightness was too dazzling for mortal eyes. We all stood there, with downcast eyes, listening spell-bound to the wonderful melody, until the chorus ceased, and the echoes, one after another, died away, and the glory faded out of the sky and the stars came back again, and no sound was heard but the faint voice of a young lamb, calling for its mother.

"The first to break the silence was my father. 'Come,' he said, in a solemn voice. 'Let us go at once to Bethlehem, and see this thing which is come to pass, which the Lord hath made known unto us.'

"So the sheep were quietly gathered into the fold at the tower, and we hastened to Bethlehem.

"It was midnight when we climbed the hill to the little city of Bethlehem; the constellation Cesil, called by the Greeks Orion, was just setting in the west. We knew not whither to go. We had only the sign of the angel by which we should know the infant Messiah. He was a babe of one day. He was lying in a manger.

" 'Let us go to the inn,' said my father. 'It stands on the very spot where King David was born. Peradventure we shall find him there.'

"Over the entrance to the court of the inn a lantern was swinging from a rope stretched across from post to post. Guided by its light, we entered, and found the courtyard full of beasts of burden, showing that the inn was crowded with travelers. In the arched shelter of the hostelry as many as could find room were lying; some who could not sleep were sitting up and waiting drearily for the morning. Two aged women near the entrance, were talking in a low tone.

" 'Peace be unto you!' said my father.

" 'The Lord be gracious unto thee,' answered the oldest woman, in a solemn voice, as she looked upon my father's white beard; 'but,' she quickly added, 'there is scanty cheer in this place for late comers.'

" 'We seek not lodging,' said my father; 'but know you whether among these guests is an infant born this day?'

" 'Verily there is,' answered the aged dame; 'a man-child more beautiful than any my eyes have ever beheld. He is lying in a manger there in the cave that serves for stable.'

"We hastened to the mouth of the cave, and there beheld our King. The oxen and the asses were lying near, and a strong man, with a grave and kind face, was leaning on his staff above the manger. A beautiful young mother lay close beside it, her cheek resting on her hands, that were clasped over the edge of the rock-hewn crib. Into this a little straw had been thrown, and over it a purple robe had been cast, whereon the infant lay. A lamp, set upon a projection of the wall of the cave, burned brightly near. The great eyes of the wonderful child were wandering about the room; his hand touched his mother's lips. I waited to hear him open his mouth and speak.

"There was a moment of silence after we entered the cave. My father broke it with his salutation:

"'Hail, thou blessed among women!' he cried. 'This child of thine is a Prince and a Saviour.'

"And then we all bowed low upon our faces before him and worshiped him with praise and gladness.

"Then my father told them all the things that we had heard and seen—the message of the angel, the song in the air, the glory of the Lord that had appeared to us—and how we had quickly come to Bethlehem, and had found things as the angel had told us.

"When my father had finished speaking, we all bowed low again before the young child; and the mother lifted him in her arms and placed his cheek against her own, smiling graciously on us, but uttering no word. And we came forth from the stable and stood again beneath the stars in the courtyard of the inn. In the early morning we came back again unto our pastures and our flocks, rejoicing to stand again in the place where the glory of God had shone and the music of heaven had filled the air."

"Come, my son, Cesil is in the south; it is midnight; let us call your father and his brother. The old man and the boy have kept their watch, and it is now time for rest."[1]

---

[1] © 1944 Meigs Publishing Co. Standard Publishing, owner. Used by permission.

A Stable Boy
A delightful Christmas story told through narrative, music, and slides. The script includes directions for making the slides.

*REFRAIN: *Sung to the tune of "Greensleeves Traditional" to set the mood. It also reappears during the narrative to allow the mood to prevail and to add a (vocal) change of pace in the narrative. (The music is published by Larrabwe Publishers, 39 W. 60th St., New York, N.Y.)*

>A Stable Boy . . . A Stable Boy,
>He was just a stable boy, you see.
>He swept the floor,
>He stacked the hay—
>He worked and worked,
>with no time for play . . .

Slide 1 **Yes, he was just a stable boy. His clothes were ragged and thread-worn, his face mostly dirty, he seldom had a pair of shoes—a wealthy traveling merchant had once given him an old pair—but they soon fell apart.

Omar, as he was called, meant "mountain-man." That was all he knew of his parents—they had been mountain people. However, the little mountain boy felt sure he was called Omar simply because it was easily yelled. It

** *Phrases underlined indicate points at which slides appear.*

seemed to Omar that surely his full name must be, "Hey you, Omar, come quickly."

2 Omar had never heard his name called so many times as in the past weeks. It seemed that the whole world had come to Bethlehem. Omar did not understand—it was all about the King's command for a new tax. Omar had asked Kaleb, the innkeeper, what it meant. Kaleb replied in a gruff voice, "Such matters are not the concern of stable boys—be about your work!"

3 Omar had risen earlier than usual, long before the daylight. It was cool in the morning hours. But there was so much work to be done Omar had not noticed the discomfort of the air.

4 There seemed no end to the line of travelers. The hotel was full—this meant but one thing to Omar—work—many donkeys and camels, the goats and sheep—all had to be fed and watered. The sun had come and gone—darkness had set in. Omar found hope of ending his long day. He had just poured a pail of water for the last donkey—all were fed and bedded down for the night. "At last," Omar thought to himself, "I, too, can bed down." Omar was looking forward to his meal of hard bread, a few dates, cheese, and goat's milk.

5 Omar looked with tired eyes at the straw piled in the southern corner of the stable. There was no wind there—it would be warm. It was not much of a bed, but it was better than sleeping in the fields. "I am so tired—" Omar muttered, "so tired." It was only a bed of straw; but to Omar it seemed like the bed of a king.

*REFRAIN

A Stable Boy

6   What was that—Omar rubbed his eyes as he sat up—he had been sound asleep. "Oh—no." "No." Omar muttered to himself. Kaleb was coming. "No, no, not another one," Omar cried in a whisper. The hotel was full—so were the stalls—there was no room—no room but Omar's bed!

7   Omar looked at the woman. She seemed very tired. She was going to be a mother—Omar could tell. He had seen too many animals not to know about such things. She was about to have a baby. She smiled at Omar. Omar felt sorry for her—but—but, it was his bed. He had worked hard. It was his bed—

8   "Kaleb had no right—no right to give my bed away," Omar mumbled to himself. He kicked the dust as he walked away from the stable towards the hills. "It is my bed—I worked for it—it is mine—even if she was tired—it is mine." "Kaleb would see," Omar thought—"He will see—there are other stables to clean—he'll see—" Omar decided he would spend the night in the hills. Tomorrow he would look for a new stable to clean. "A stable is a stable, what difference does it make which one you clean?"

9   Omar had walked for an hour or more. He was near the top of the large hill just south of the city. Omar was troubled. He was sad and angry. Kaleb shouldn't have taken his bed. Yet, Omar did feel sorry for the woman—she was so pretty and so tired. There were tears in his eyes—Omar was not sure why he was crying.

10   Omar turned and looked toward Bethlehem. As he did, his eyes opened wide—"What is that?" Omar had seen many stars in his young life, but never one like that. What could it mean? It shone in the heavens like a torch—like a ball of fire. It was right over the city. "What could it mean?"

Omar had once overheard a very wise man talking with the innkeeper about stars. He had told Kaleb if he ever saw a giant and very bright star in the sky, that it would be a sign of a very, very important thing. "Could this be the star he spoke of?" Omar wondered—

11 Omar ran back towards Bethlehem. He would follow the star, he thought. His feet moved faster and faster—Suddenly he seemed to be standing right under it. Omar leaned back and peered straight up at the star. Omar heard the bray of a donkey. He looked around. He could not believe it—he was standing right in front of the stable. He was right back where he had started from. The star had led him back to the stable—Why?

12 Omar crept to the stable window and peered in. There was a group of shepherds—Kaleb and his wife—and some of the hotel guests—they were all smiling and whispering. They huddled around the south corner of the stable— around the straw bed.

13 Omar moved to peek through a crack in the wall. He saw a baby. "A baby," Omar whispered, "a baby." A baby was lying on Omar's bed—Omar was glad his bed was out of the wind; the baby would be warm.

14 "Omar," a voice called—"there you are." Omar turned to see Kaleb. Kaleb put his arm around Omar—this was the first time he had ever done that. He walked Omar close to the baby.
"Look, Omar, look at the baby. Did you see the star? It is for him—for the baby."

15 "Is he the one?" the shepherds asked, smiling at Omar. "Yes," replied the woman, "he is the one who gave his bed to the baby."

A Stable Boy 35

"God will bless you, my boy," the shepherd said.
"Yes," the woman added—"God bless you."
"Yes, God bless you," said Kaleb—"God bless you, Omar."

*Refrain

16 Omar did not understand what they meant, but he was glad he had come back. He was also glad no one knew he had been angry about giving up his bed. As Omar looked at the baby, he was not angry any more—no, not at all. He was glad—glad the baby had his bed. It was kind-of-like a gift. "Yes," Omar thought to himself, "it is a gift, little one—my gift to you at your birth." The thought of giving to the baby made Omar feel good.

"What is the baby's name?" Omar asked.

"His name?" the woman replied. "He will be called JESUS."

"Jesus,"—"Jesus," Omar thought to himself—"Jesus." Omar knew what that name meant—"Jesus means Jehova is Salvation—the one who saves." "What a nice name," Omar thought, "Jesus, the one who helps and saves."

*Refrain

> A stable boy, a stable boy;
> He was just a stable boy, you see.
> But in his bed, of straw and hay,
> Christ, the Lord was born.

Suggestions for Preparing Abstract Slides

Note: These instructions are for making abstract slides to be used with "A Stable Boy." If you have a steady hand, a little imagination, and the willingness to try, you have the secret of producing "homemade" abstract slides.

Materials:

1. A sharp pair of scissors and a razor blade.
2. Empty standard 2″ x 2″ 35-mm slide frames.

3. A variety of colored cellophane paper.
4. Sheets of heavy paper or thin cardboard and/or old Christmas cards.
5. Pencil or pen.
6. Glue and transparent tape.

Steps:
1. Select the slide scenes you desire to use. There are 16 suggested scenes.
2. Draw (or trace from a Christmas card, etc.) the silhouette outline of each of the desired scenes on the cardboard or paper. You must draw the scene within a 1½" x 1½" area on the paper. Now cut out the silhouette scene. (You can also get the results you want by cutting appropriate miniature scenes from Christmas cards, etc. These must fit within the dimensions of 1½" x 1½".)
3. Take the 2" x 2" slide frame apart. (Slice the frame into two halves with a razor blade.)
4. Place the silhouette scene between the two halves. Check the fit. Trim edges of the scene to fit the slide frame evenly.
5. Glue the bottom edge of the silhouette scene to the bottom edge of one frame half.
6. Decide what color effect you want for this slide scene. (Yellow, blue, red or some combination of colors.) Cut the selected cellophane paper to fit evenly within your frame. Place your paper on one frame half and glue down all edges.
7. Take both slide frame halves and glue them back together. Your slide is now finished. Repeat the process with each desired slide scene.

NOTE: You can vary the coloring effects by using combinations of colored cellophane paper and by making any given area of the cellophane covering thicker than other areas.

You can add special effects such as a "star" over the silhouette by making a small pin puncture in the cellophane paper used as the sky.

You can use slides made by the above directions in any standard 35-mm slide projector. After making one slide, place it in a 35-mm projector and study your results. With study and

A Stable Boy

effort you can achieve a variety of effects in "homemade" abstract slides.

Suggested Slides

Slide 1   A thin boy poorly and shabbily dressed.
Slide 2   Scene of travelers arriving at "an inn."
Slide 3   "Omar" carrying buckets of hay, etc.
Slide 4   "Omar" at work, leading an animal.
Slide 5   A "straw bed" in the corner of a "stable."
Slide 6   "Omar" sitting up in his bed.
Slide 7   A silhouette of an expectant mother, "Mary."
Slide 8   "Omar" walking into hills, kicking his foot in the dust.
Slide 9   "Omar" looking from a hilltop back toward Bethlehem.
Slide 10 "Outline" view of Bethlehem with stars and one "bright star" over the city.
Slide 11 "Omar" running or standing looking up at the "star."
Slide 12 "Omar" looking into window seeing crowd inside.
Slide 13 Scene "Omar" sees inside, the Baby in his bed.
Slide 14 "Omar" and "Kaleb"—"Kaleb" is leading "Omar" through the door of the stable.
Slide 15 Scene of the people inside the stable.
Slide 16 Scene of "Baby" in "Omar's" bed with crowd and "Omar" around him.

The Miracle

A short Christmas play in three scenes, using modern theme and dress. Requires little staging, costuming, and properties. Suited for classroom or church auditorium use. As many extras as desired can be used in singing, etc.

TIME: *Present* AGE GROUP: *Young teens*

PURPOSE: *To show the need of presenting the real meaning of Christmas.*

SETTING: *Choir practice room of a church, Scene I. Girls walking home, Scene II. Living room of an apartment, Scene III.*

CHARACTERS: MARY CAROL
 THERESA JEANNE MOORE
 SUSAN MRS. MOORE
 ALICE RANDY
 MAID KAY
 MRS. WALTON, *choir leader*

Scene I

MARY: I'm glad practice is over. (*Girls begin gathering coats, scarves, etc., to go home.*) Say, Susan, what are you getting for Christmas?

SUSAN: Oh, I'm not sure. I know what I want, though. I saw

a beautiful watch in Mr. Jenkins' show window. It's got little diamonds all around its face.

ALICE: I'll bet it costs a fortune. I wouldn't expect my folks to put that much into a gift for me. But I do want a new cashmere sweater. Anything in the clothes category suits my folks. If I ask for it, I'll get that sweater.

CAROL: I already know what I'll get. My folks started my luggage set last year. The only surprise I'll have is trying to guess which piece I'll get this year. (*Looks disgusted.*)

KAY: You never can tell, Carol. Maybe they'll put a bunch of surprises inside the luggage. Santa knows you've been good this year.

CAROL: That would really be a surprise! You haven't said anything about your plans, Jeanne. What will you get for Christmas?

JEANNE (*has been sitting off to herself during practice. She joins the girls as they get ready to go.*): Mama will give me a check next week and I'll pick out whatever I want.

KAY: Doesn't your church have a Christmas program? (*All girls look surprised at Jeanne's attitude.*)

JEANNE: Huh, Are you kidding? This is the first time I've been inside a church in years, except to Aunt Lera's funeral. Mother said then she felt like she was smothering to death.

ALICE: Christmas is something special at our house. Don't you and your mother do anything different at Christmas time, Jeanne?

JEANNE (*shrugs*): Not really, except sleep late, and go out for dinner.

KAY: Boy, we have company, and lots of extra food and oodles of fun at Christmas. And, of course, we have special services at church. And presents galore!

JEANNE: Sure, that's the most important part of Christmas, isn't it? All Christmas is, is getting lots of gifts, sometimes from people you hardly even know. It's really foolish to waste your time on a racket that just gives more money to the business people.

CAROL: Have you always believed like that, Jeanne?

JEANNE (*quietly*): Not always. We used to—pretend along with everyone else at Christmas. That was before Daddy left. He really loved Christmas, but Mother says that was a big show just like everything else he did. So she says Christmas is foolish. I guess it would take a real miracle to change her mind about Christmas.

M. WALTON: I think you girls had better be going now. It's late. Don't forget our next practice. (*Girls leave, calling good-bye to the teacher.*)

Scene II

(*Girls are walking home from school. The only two left together are* MARY *and* THERESA.)

MARY: I feel awful about Jeanne. She's such a sweet girl. It must be terrible not to like Christmas. We've always enjoyed this time of the year so much.

THERESA: I'm sorry for her, too. They've got lots of money, but little happiness. But, Mary, the thing that bothers me most is that we have helped Jeanne to be like that.

MARY: You must be crazy! What are you talking about?

THERESA: Well, don't you know that we call ourselves Christians, but how many times has Jeanne heard us even mention the name of Christ when we've talked about Christmas?

MARY (*surprised*): You sure said it, girl! We haven't talked about much except what we want to get for Christmas. I guess we've fitted right into Jeanne's picture of people at Christmas. We sure haven't been a very good witness, have we?

THERESA: No, we haven't, but I've been thinking about something, Mary. Maybe we couldn't exactly work a miracle for Jeanne, but we might be able to show her and Mrs. Moore that Christmas isn't all bad. But we'll have to hurry. We'll have to call Mrs. Walton and see if she'll help us. Come on, I'll tell you my plan over some hot chocolate at our house.

MARY: Sounds crazy, but wonderful! Let's go! (*Girls hurry off together.*)

Scene III

(*Living room of an apartment. The girls stand in a doorway with* MRS. WALTON, *talking to a* MAID. *They carry packages and sacks with a small tree, decorations, etc., in them.*)

MAID: Are you sure you are at the right apartment?

MARY: Oh, yes. We are friends of Jeanne. She had to practice a program at school and I'm sure she'll be home soon. We'd appreciate your letting us wait here for her.

MAID: Yes, I'm sure they'll be home very soon. They never go anywhere except work and school, hardly. They'll come straight home.

THERESA (*whispers to* MRS. WALTON *and girls*): Maybe we could let her in on our plans.

GIRLS: Yes, let's tell her.

THERESA: Well, you see, we want Jeanne and her mother to have a *real* Christmas this year. Jeanne says her mother hates Christmas and we thought we'd help her like it again.

MAID: Well, I never thought I'd see the day. I didn't know there were young people left in this world like you. Come right on in and do whatever you need to do.

MARY: Thank you. We'll have to work fast now, girls. We'll have to be through before Jeanne and her mother come. (*The* GIRLS *and* MRS. WALTON *get busy, decorating a little tree with lights, etc.*)

MAID: Isn't that beautiful? I don't believe I've ever seen a prettier tree. I sure hope your idea works. I've helped Mrs. Moore for years now, and she and Jeanne haven't seen much happiness since Mr. Moore left them.

RANDY: Maybe we could be sure about our idea if we prayed about it before they got here.

M. WALTON: Yes, Randy, would you lead us in prayer? (*The girls bow their heads.*)

RANDY: Dear Lord, we need your help. We haven't been very good examples of Christians because we haven't told Jeanne the real meaning of Christmas. Please give us this chance to show Jeanne that Christmas is a time of love and sharing, not just of getting gifts. Amen.

KAY: We'd better hide. They should be here right away.
(*Everyone scampers to a hiding place. The* MAID *turns out the lights except those on the tree. She stands out of sight near the door.*)

MAID: Sh-h-h. I hear them coming now.

(JEANNE *and her* MOTHER *are talking. They open the door and are surprised.*)

M. MOORE: What in the world has happened?

JEANNE: Oh, Mother, did you do this?

The Miracle 43

M. Moore: You know I didn't do any such a thing, Jeanne. Rose! Are you responsible for this—this junk!

Maid: No, ma'am. I didn't do it, but it sure is pretty, isn't it?

Jeanne: Mother, come here! These gifts have our names on them. This tree is beautiful. This angel at the top makes the whole room glow. Where did it come from?

M. Moore: I can't imagine. Everybody I know has a good idea about my attitude toward Christmas.

(*The young people stand quietly and begin singing "Silent Night." Mrs. Moore sits down in chair and puts her head in her hands. Jeanne stands in amazement as her friends sing. They begin singing "Away in a Manger" after one verse of "Silent Night."*)

Jeanne: I don't know what to say. I thought I didn't like Christmas. Maybe I just didn't know what it was all about.

M. Walton: Here is a book that will tell you all about Chrismas, Mrs. Moore. (*Hands her a Bible.*) Your friends bought this for you. It will tell you the meaning of life all year long.

M. Moore: Have I been wrong? (*Cries softly.*)

Jeanne: Oh, Mother, go ahead and cry. I feel like crying, too. Is Christmas really so bad? Couldn't we celebrate just this one time since the stuff is already here?

Maid: It would be a shame to throw all this pretty stuff away, Mrs. Moore. You've seen a real miracle tonight.

M. Moore: I guess I have seen a miracle. I had forgotten the real meaning of Christmas. These last six years have made me so bitter that I didn't want to think of joy and happiness and giving presents. But, I have been wrong. Jeanne, I'm sorry I've robbed you of so much happiness. And we won't celebrate Christmas just this year. I promise you that from now on we'll try to keep the meaning of Christmas all year long. (*Hugs* JEANNE.)

(*The young people begin singing "O Come, All Ye Faithful" and* MARY *takes* JEANNE *by the hand and invites her to join. Slowly at first, then loud and clear,* JEANNE *and her* MOTHER *sing with them.*)

Tell It Again

In this program, the traditional Christmas story is told by AUNT MARTHA *in a contemporary home setting. The major events in the story are portrayed in biblical tableaux.*

(*The five people involved in the home scene enter, moving at a good pace. All except* JULIE *go to the extreme right side of the platform where the home scene is set up. They freeze [remain motionless] with their backs to the audience.* JULIE *simultaneously moves to the center of the platform and speaks directly to the audience.*)

JULIE: Hello there! Welcome to our Christmas program. We hope you like it.

We're not using any special scenery, so we'll count on you to use your imagination.

Over here (*points to her left and moves to the extreme left side of the platform*) will be a field with shepherds watching their sheep—not just a field and shepherds—but also many other places and people—if our imagination really works.

Over there (*points to the home scene and moves back to the center of the platform as she speaks*) is the den in my home. That's Aunt Martha, my mother's aunt. (AUNT MARTHA *turns and sits, facing the audience. So do the other characters as their names are called.*) That's my brother Tom, my sister Emily, and Rudy, a boy who lives two streets over from us. Oh, I forgot to tell you—I'm Julie.

Well, it's time to get started. (*She walks over to join the others.*)

SPOTLIGHT: *Dim out or turn off the overhead lights and focus the spotlight on the home scene.*

TOM: Aunt Martha, I brought Rudy. He says he's never heard the Christmas story.

AUNT MARTHA: Well, we're glad to have Rudy, aren't we? Rudy, what I'm going to tell you about happened long, long ago. It happened to Mary, a young Jewish girl, perhaps not many years older than Julie. She was engaged to be married to a young man named Joseph. One day when she was alone, an angel appeared, and spoke to her. At first, she couldn't believe what he told her.

SPOTLIGHT: *Off of home scene and upon* MARY *and the angel,* GABRIEL.

ANGEL: "Hail, thou that art highly favoured, the Lord is with thee: blessed art thou among women.

(MARY *reacts with fright.*)

"Fear not, Mary: for thou hast found favour with God. And, behold, thou shalt conceive in thy womb, and bring forth a son, and shalt call his name Jesus. He shall be great, and shall be called the Son of the Highest: . . . and of his kingdom there shall be no end."

MARY: But how can this be? I have no husband.

ANGEL: "The Holy Ghost shall come upon thee, and the power of the Highest shall overshadow thee: therefore also that holy thing which shall be born of thee shall be called the Son of God.

"And, behold, thy cousin Elisabeth, she hath also conceived a son in her old age: and this is the sixth month with her, who was called barren.

"For with God nothing shall be impossible."

MARY: "Behold the handmaid of the Lord; be it unto me according to thy word."

SPOTLIGHT: *Off of MARY and the ANGEL and upon the home scene.*

EMILY: What's a handmaid, Aunt Martha?

AUNT MARTHA: Well, it really means slave. Though Mary didn't understand it all, she loved God and said she would willingly be his servant.

   Mary just had to tell somebody the exciting news, so she went to the home of her cousin, Elisabeth, as fast as she could go to tell what had happened.

SPOTLIGHT: *Off of home scene and upon MARY and ELISABETH.*

MARY (*running to ELISABETH and embracing her*): Elisabeth!
ELISABETH: Mary!
   "Blessed art thou among women, and blessed is the fruit of thy womb."

MARY: "My soul doth magnify the Lord, and my spirit hath rejoiced in God my Saviour. For he hath regarded the low estate of his handmaiden! For, behold, from henceforth all generations shall call me blessed. For he that is mighty hath done to me great things; and holy is his name."

SPOTLIGHT: *Off of MARY and ELISABETH and upon home scene.*

AUNT MARTHA: Mary stayed with her cousin Elisabeth, about three months. Then she returned to her own home.

   When Joseph, the young man Mary was engaged to marry, heard the news about Mary, he was troubled. He was a good man and did not want to make a public example of Mary.

   While he was trying to decide what to do, an angel appeared to him in a dream.

SPOTLIGHT: *Off of home scene and upon JOSEPH, who is asleep.*

ANGEL: "Joseph, thou son of David, fear not to take unto thee Mary thy wife: for that which is conceived in her is of the Holy Ghost. And she shall bring forth a son, and thou shalt call his name JESUS: for he shall save his people from their sins."

SPOTLIGHT: *Off of angel and* JOSEPH *and upon home scene.*

AUNT MARTHA: When Joseph woke up, he did what the angel told him, and brought Mary home to be his wife.

About that time, Caesar Augustus, the Roman Emperor, decided that a census should be taken throughout the nation.

Joseph had to go to Bethlehem for the census, so Mary went with him.

"While they were there, the time came for her baby to be born; and she gave birth to her first child, a son. She wrapped him in a blanket and laid him in a manger, because there was no room for them in the village inn."

SPOTLIGHT: *Off of home scene and upon Nativity.*

MUSIC: "Gentle Mary Laid Her Child," *stanza 1*
"Silent Night," *stanzas 1 and 2*

SPOTLIGHT: *Off the Nativity and upon home scene.*

AUNT MARTHA: "That night some shepherds were in the fields outside the village, guarding their flocks of sheep. Suddenly, an angel appeared among them, and the landscape shone bright with the glory of the Lord. They were badly frightened."

SPOTLIGHT: *Off of the home scene and upon the shepherds.*

MUSIC: "While Shepherds Watched Their Flocks," *stanza 1*

ANGEL: "Fear not: for, behold, I bring you good tidings of great joy, which shall be to all people. For unto you is born this day in the city of David a Saviour, which is Christ the Lord.

And this shall be a sign unto you; Ye shall find the babe wrapped in swaddling clothes, lying in a manger."

AUNT MARTHA (*in the darkness*): And all of a sudden the angel was joined by many other angels, praising God.

(*Several* ANGELS *enter during* AUNT MARTHA's *foregoing speech. All the angels speak with animation and joy.*)

ANGELS: "Glory to God in the highest, and on earth peace, good will toward men."

MUSIC: "While Shepherds Watched Their Flocks," *stanzas 3 and 5*

SPOTLIGHT: *Off the* SHEPHERDS *and* ANGELS *and upon the home scene.*

AUNT MARTHA: When the angels had gone back to heaven, the shepherds said to each other, "'Come on! Let's go to Bethlehem! Let's see this wonderful thing that has happened, which the Lord has told us about.'

"They ran to the village and found their way to Mary and Joseph. And there was the baby, lying in the manger!"

SPOTLIGHT: *Off the home scene and upon the Nativity with* MARY, JOSEPH, *and the* SHEPHERDS.

MUSIC: "Angels from the Realms of Glory," *stanzas 1 and 2*

SPOTLIGHT: *Off the Nativity and upon the home scene.*

AUNT MARTHA: "Then the shepherds went back to their fields and flocks again, praising God for the visit of the angels and because they had seen the child, just as the angels had told them they would."

A few days later, Joseph and Mary took the baby Jesus to Jerusalem to present him to the Lord.

"That day a man named Simeon, who lived in Jerusalem, was in the Temple. He was a good man, very devout, filled with the Holy Spirit and constantly expecting the Messiah to come soon.

"For the Holy Spirit had revealed to him that he would not die until he had seen him—God's anointed King.

"The Holy Spirit had impelled him to go to the Temple that day; and so, when Mary and Joseph arrived to present the baby Jesus to the Lord in obedience to the law, Simeon was there and took him in his arms, praising God."

SPOTLIGHT: *Off the home scene and upon* SIMEON, *holding the baby Jesus.*

SIMEON: "Lord, now lettest thou thy servant depart in peace, according to thy word: for mine eyes have seen thy salvation, which thou hast prepared before the face of all people; a light to lighten the Gentiles and the glory of the people of Israel."

SPOTLIGHT: *Off of* SIMEON *and upon the home scene.*

AUNT MARTHA: When Jesus was born, some Wise Men came from far away to Jerusalem. They said, "Where is the newborn King of the Jews? for we have seen his star in far-off eastern lands, and have come to worship him."

King Herod was deeply troubled by their questions. He secretly sent for them and said, "Go to Bethlehem . . . and search for the child. And when you find him, come back and tell me, so that I can worship him too!"

The Wise Men listened to the king and then left. The bright star they had seen in the east appeared again. It went before them to Bethlehem and led them to the place where the young child was.

They went into the house where the baby and his mother were and fell down on the floor and worshipped him. Then they gave him gold, frankincense, and myrrh.

SPOTLIGHT: *Off the home scene and upon* THREE KINGS.

THREE KINGS: "We Three Kings"
(*They walk across the front of the church auditorium, singing "We Three Kings" as they move to the platform*

Tell It Again   51

where MARY *and the* BABY JESUS *are. Time the walking so that they reach the steps leading up to the platform by the end of the first chorus. Let the one who brought gold sing his solo and move on to* MARY *and* JESUS *as he sings. Let him kneel and present his gift as the other two join with him in singing the chorus. The* SECOND KING *sings the third stanza and moves to the platform. He too kneels on the chorus and offers his gift. The* THIRD KING *approaches on verse four. All three sing the fifth stanza, still kneeling.)*

SPOTLIGHT: *Off the* KINGS *and* MARY *and upon the home scene.*

AUNT MARTHA: In a dream, God told the kings that they should not return to Herod, so they went home a different way.
After they were gone, Joseph dreamed again. In his dream, an angel appeared to him.

SPOTLIGHT: *Off the home scene and upon* JOSEPH *and the* ANGEL.

ANGEL: "Arise, and take the young child and his mother, and flee into Egypt, and be thou there until I bring thee word: for Herod will seek the young child to destroy him."

SPOTLIGHT: *Off of* JOSEPH *and the* ANGEL *and upon the home scene.*

AUNT MARTHA: "That same night he left for Egypt with Mary and the baby, and stayed there until King Herod's death."
King Herod was furious when he found out that the Wise Men had deceived him, so he sent soldiers to Bethlehem and ordered them to kill every boy baby they could find that was two years old or under. The Wise Men had told Herod that the star appeared to them two years before.
When Herod died, an angel of the Lord appeared in a dream to Joseph in Egypt, and told him to take the baby and his mother back to Israel. On the way home, God spoke to Joseph in another dream and told him not to go to Jerusalem, so they went to Galilee instead and lived in Nazareth.

So, God kept on protecting the baby Jesus—because he had something very special for him to do! I'll tell you that part of the story another time.

Tom: See, Rudy—didn't I tell you it was a great story?

Rudy: Is it all truly real?

Aunt Martha: Yes, Rudy, it's all truly real!

Rudy: Tell it again—to my mother and little sister!

Aunt Martha: Sure! Come on, we'll go tell it to your mother and little sister—and everybody else who'll listen!

(*They exit down the steps and out. The* Pastor *closes the service.*)

Staging Directions

Platform Arrangement

Arrange the home scene as far to the right side (stage right) of the platform as possible. A couple chairs will be sufficient furniture to suggest a home.

Place the biblical tableaux at the left side of the platform as far removed from the home scene as possible.

The shepherd scene can be played in the choir loft area, with the angels in the baptistry.

The Tableaux

Elevate the tableaux so that each character can easily be seen. Work for an informal grouping of the people in the home scene, with some sitting on the floor.

See "How-to Instructions" for arranging tableaux.

The Storyteller

Choose the best storyteller available to play the role of Aunt Martha. Put the script in her hands at least six weeks ahead so she can learn the story and really make it live. Be sure that she and the others who speak can be heard. If microphones are to be used, rehearse with them several times.

Costuming, Lighting, Make-up, Scenery

"How-to Instructions" will be helpful here.

All Scripture references except those used in biblical scenes are from *Living Gospels*, Kenneth N. Taylor, ed. (Wheaton, Ill., Tyndale House, Publishers). Used by permission.

Whose Birthday Is It, Anyway?

In this program, the Christmas story is told through a puppet play. It is appropriate for use with children or with the entire church.

(*The puppet play begins with all overhead lights on.*)

Biff (*yelling*): Help, help—get me out of here—get me out of here!

Puppet No. 2 (*appears*): Where are you? Where are you? (*As he speaks, he looks for* Biff. Biff *keeps hollering for help.* Puppet No. 2 *finds* Biff *and pulls him up where he can be seen by the audience.*)

Biff: Thanks for pulling me out of that miserable box.

Puppet No. 2: Never mind. I must be on my way. See you later.

Biff: Good-bye—and thanks again!

(Biff *turns and speaks directly to the audience.*) Oh, the life of a puppet! I sometimes wish I'd been a *fish* instead.

That day when Billy finished making me, he said, "You're Biff—that's who you are, you're Biff. And you'll be the *star* in our very next puppet play!" A star—in a play! I *couldn't* believe it. I clapped my hands and skipped about with joy.

Billy took me to his room and put me on a table near his bed. We had such fun together! But one day I fell down behind the bed. I found myself stuck between the wall and the bed. I kicked and wiggled, I pushed and pulled—but nothing happened. I still was stuck there for ever so long! But one morning while Billy was at school, his mother decided to give his room a *good* cleaning. She moved the bed away from the wall and started sweeping. All of a sudden, she saw me.

"Well there's Biff," she said to herself. "Billy's been looking all over for him. I'll put him away so Billy will know where he is."

She picked me up, dusted me off, and stuffed me in a box. She closed the lid real tight and put me in a closet.

Now have you ever been stuffed in a box and put on a high shelf in a closet? It's dark and scary—and it's hard to breathe all cramped up.

BILLY (*speaking off stage*): Mom, if Sammy calls, tell him I'll be right back.

BIFF: That's Billy. I'll hide and surprise him. (BIFF *disappears from view.* BILLY *enters whistling. When he gets near,* BIFF *pops up and speaks.*)

BIFF: *Surprise!*

BILLY: Biff! I've looked everywhere for you. Where have you been?

BIFF: In the closet, crammed down in a box. Your mother put me there so you'd know where I was.

BILLY: And she forgot to tell me about it.

BIFF: You know, mothers can't think of *everything*.

BILLY: Well, I'm glad I found you, Biff. I have something *big* I need you to help me do.

BIFF: Oh? What is it?

BILLY: A play—a real important play.

BIFF: What's it about?

BILLY: It's a story you haven't heard, Biff. It's about a king who was born in a manger.

BIFF: In a manger? What's a manger?

BILLY: It's a—well, it's a place where they feed cows.

BIFF: A king—born where they feed cows?

BILLY: Yes, that's what the play is about. I'll tell you the whole story when I get back. I have to run an errand for Mom now. See you in a few minutes, Biff!
(BILLY *exits, going out the opposite direction from which he came.* BIFF *watches him go and then hops about with joy.*)

BIFF: A play! A play! Biff, in a play! You know—maybe the life of a puppet isn't so bad after all. (*He exits.*)

MUSIC: "Silent Night" or one of the other traditional carols. (*Use recorded music if possible. Have the record player and the person who operates it unseen. As the song concludes, dim out or turn off the overhead lights.*)

Scene II

SPOTLIGHT: *Upon puppet stage.*
(BILLY *enters and stands at the side of the puppet stage as he speaks.*)

BILLY: Everything all set, Biff?

BIFF (*unseen*): All set!

BILLY: Then I'm turning it over to you. I'll be sitting right here on the front row if you need me.
(*He walks to the front row and sits. As he moves, play a few measures of the carol previously used. Fade it out as* BIFF *enters followed by* BING.)

BING: Biff, may I ask you a question?

BIFF: Of course. What is it?

BING: Oh, I can't. You'll think I'm the *dumbest* puppet you ever met!

BIFF: Of course I won't. Go ahead. There are things *I* don't know.

BING: (*shocked to find out that* BIFF *doesn't know everything*): Really?

BIFF: Sure!

BING: My question is about all the rushing around at our house—the buying of gifts, decorating, and cooking. I heard them say they're trying to get ready for Christmas. Biff, what's Christmas?

BIFF: It's really a—kind of—celebration, Bing—a birthday celebration, in honor of someone very important.

BING: Oh?

BIFF: Want me to tell you all about it?

BING: Oh, please do, Biff.

BIFF: Well, the story (and it's a true one) is in a book called the Bible. A young Jewish girl was alone one day when an angel from heaven spoke to her.

SPOTLIGHT: *Off of* BIFF *and* BING *and upon* MARY *and the* ANGEL *who have taken their positions in the darkness.*

ANGEL: O, honored one, "The Lord is with you. Don't be frightened, Mary, for God has decided to wonderfully bless you!" You are going to have a baby, "And you are to name him Jesus. He shall be very great and shall be called the Son of God." God will make him a King and his kingdom shall never end.

MARY: But how can this be? I have no husband.

ANGEL: "In the power of God your son will be born, for he is the Son of God."*

MARY: "I am the Lord's servant, and I am willing to do whatever He says."

SPOTLIGHT: *Off the ANGEL and MARY and upon BIFF and BING.*

BIFF: Mary was puzzled at what the angel told her. She was engaged to be married to a young man named Joseph. What would he think? What would he do? About this time, an angel appeared to Joseph, in a dream.

SPOTLIGHT: *Off of BIFF and BING and upon JOSEPH and the angel.*

ANGEL: "Joseph, son of David, don't hesitate to take Mary as your wife! For the child within her has been conceived by the Holy Spirit!

"And she will have a son, and you shall name Him Jesus (meaning 'Savior'), for He will save His people from their sins."

SPOTLIGHT: *Off of JOSEPH and the ANGEL and upon BIFF and BING.*

BIFF: "When Joseph awoke, he did as the angel commanded, and brought Mary home to be his wife."

Before the baby was born, the Roman Emperor, Augustus, ordered a census taken. Everyone had to register in his family's hometown. Joseph had to travel to Bethlehem and he took Mary with him.

"Bethlehem was so crowded that they could find no place to stay, so they had to sleep in a stable. That was where the baby was born, and Mary made a bed for Him in a manger."*

SPOTLIGHT: *Off of BIFF and BING and upon NATIVITY.*

MUSIC: *"Away in a Manger"*

SPOTLIGHT: *Off the* NATIVITY *and upon* BIFF *and* BING.

BIFF: That night some shepherds were in the fields outside of the village, watching their sheep. Suddenly, an angel appeared to them and they were frightened.

SPOTLIGHT: *Off of* BING *and* BIFF *and upon the* SHEPHERDS.

MUSIC: *"While Shepherds Watched Their Flocks," stanza 1*

ANGEL: "Don't be afraid! I bring you the most joyful news ever announced, and it is for everyone!
"The Savior—yes, the Messiah, the Lord—has been born tonight in Bethlehem! How will you recognize him? You will find a baby wrapped in a blanket, lying in a manger!" (*Other Angels join the one.*)

ANGELS: "Glory to God in the highest,
On earth peace,
Good will among men."

SPOTLIGHT: *Off the* SHEPHERDS *and upon* BIFF *and* BING.

BIFF: After the angels were gone, the shepherds said to each other, "'Come on! Let's go to Bethlehem! Let's see this wonderful thing that has happened, which the Lord has told us about.' They ran to the village and found their way to Mary and Joseph. And there was the baby, lying in the manger."

SPOTLIGHT: *Off of* BIFF *and* BING *and upon the* NATIVITY *with the* SHEPHERDS *added.*

MUSIC: *"Gentle Mary Laid Her Child"*

SPOTLIGHT: *Off of* MARY, JOSEPH, *and the* SHEPHERDS *and upon* BIFF *and* BING.

BIFF: "They told everyone they met what the angels had said, and they went back to the fields thanking God for what they had heard and seen.

"When the baby was eight days old, Mary and Joseph gave him his name, Jesus. And when he was forty days old they took him to Jerusalem. For the first boy baby in every Jewish family was carried to the Temple, with a sacrifice gift to God.

"There was an old, old man named Simeon who wanted more than anything to see the Saviour God had promised to send to his people. And somehow he knew that God would let him live long enough to see the Saviour with his own eyes.

"One day Simeon felt that God wanted him to go to the Temple. So when Mary and Joseph and the baby came in, he was waiting. He saw Jesus, and he reached out his arms to hold him, for he knew this was the Saviour. As he held the baby in his arms he thanked God for answering his prayers."*

SPOTLIGHT: *Off of* BIFF *and* BING *and upon* SIMEON *holding* BABY JESUS.

SIMEON: "Lord, now your servant is ready to go,
For I have seen your Gift,
Just as you promised to send him,
The Gift you have been making ready
For all the world,
The Light to guide the people of Israel,
And the people of all the world."*

SPOTLIGHT: *Off of* SIMEON *and upon* BIFF *and* BING.

BIFF: And that's the story of Christmas, Bing!

BING: A *beautiful* story, Biff! But—you know—I'm afraid the people at my house have never heard it.

BIFF: Really?

BING: I don't believe they know whose birthday it is, Biff. They're showering each other with lots of gifts, but I've never heard them mention the name of Jesus. *I don't believe they know whose birthday it is!*

BIFF: Why don't you tell them?

BING: Me?

BIFF: Yes, you! Why not?

BING: Well—er—well, why not? Thanks, Biff, for telling *me* about Christmas. I'd better get moving! I see that I have a very important job to do. Good-bye, Biff.

BIFF: So long, Bing!
(BING *exits.* BIFF *turns his head in thought and then speaks to himself.*)

BIFF: What was it Bing said—"I don't believe they know whose birthday it is." Huh, that's something to think about!! Maybe lots of people don't know whose birthday it is. (*He speaks directly to the audience on the last line.*) Say, why don't YOU tell them? (*He exits.*)

STAGING DIRECTIONS

Making the Puppets

The puppets can be made and operated by older children, youth, or adults. The play can be presented just for children, or it can be done before the entire church. When it is presented in the church auditorium or in some other large place, use youth or adults to manipulate the puppets and to do the speaking. It will be difficult for children to be heard in a large room.

There are many types of puppets that could be used for the play. One of the simplest can be made out of Styrofoam.

Begin with a Styrofoam ball 3" in diameter. (Use a larger size if the play is to be done in the church auditorium.) With glue-all or some other recommended adhesive, fasten facial features onto the Styrofoam ball. These can be cut out of felt, construction paper, or any type of scrap material available. Fashion the hair from crepe paper or yarn.

With a pencil, punch a hole in the Styrofoam ball where the

puppet's neck will be. Use the index finger to enlarge the hole until it fits the finger snugly.

From a three-inch square of light cardboard, roll and glue a tube that will fit the hole you have made. Push the tube up into the hole and glue it in place. Leave about an inch protruding for the puppet's neck. His costume can be glued to the neck.

Costumes can be made of crepe paper or cloth. A simple biblical tunic can be quickly made from a piece of cloth about thirty inches long and six to eight inches wide. (The width will depend upon the size of the person's hand who will operate the puppet.)

Fold the material lengthwise in half. Let the fold be the top and the open end the bottom. Sew, staple, or glue the two sides. Leave enough opening on each side for the puppet's arms. (These will be made by the operator's thumb and little finger.) Leave the bottom of the tunic open to put the arm up through. Cut a hole at the center of the top, folded edge, just large enough for the neck tube of the puppet to go through. Glue the tunic onto the neck.

When the arm has been put up through the tunic, tie a sash around the middle of the costume. A headpiece can be fastened on with straight pins or with glue.

Rehearsals

In rehearsals, decide where each person will be backstage and what motions the puppet will make as he talks. Practice moving the puppets so they will not get in each other's way.

Make the puppet's actions express something, rather than just jiggling him around. Work before a mirror so you can see what effects you're creating.

Create dramatic illusion by hiding the puppeteer so that the puppet appears to be moving independently on its own.

Be sure that the costume of the puppet is long enough to cover the hand and wrist of the operator.

Every action of the puppet should be bold and distinct.

Only the character who's speaking moves. The other puppets stay still and focus their attention on him.

The Puppet Stage

An elaborate stage is not necessary. In a children's department it can be as simple as a table turned on its side with the puppeteers working from behing the table. A colored bed sheet hung between two coatracks will make a good stage. In the church auditorium, the choir rail may be a perfect stage.

Be sure the puppets are up high enough to be seen.

The Dialogue

Usually, the chief weakness of puppet plays is that the dialogue cannot be heard and understood. Use microphones when working in a large space.

Use two people for each puppet that has a speaking part. Let one of them do the dialogue and let the other one operate the puppet. This will divide the responsibility and result in a better presentation.

Lighting

An effectve spotlight can be improvised by the use of a slide projector. See "How-to Instructions."

---

* These references are from *The Bible Story Book* by Bethann Van Ness, Broadman Press, Nashville, Tennessee. Used by permission.

Other quotations are from *Living Gospels*, Kenneth N. Taylor, ed. (Wheaton, Ill.: Tyndale House, Publishers).

White Christmas

This program is woven around Tolstoi's beautiful story, "Where Love Is, There God Is Also." The entire congregation becomes involved in sharing their love as they bring to the front of the church gifts, wrapped in white, to be shared with people in need.

(After singing some of the traditional carols, make necessary announcements. Establish a worship atmosphere by singing, "O Come, All Ye Faithful," followed by the offering.)

SOLO: "Thou Didst Leave Thy Throne"

(At the close of the solo, the ORGANIST plays a few measures as the SPEECH CHOIR moves into place.)

BOY 1: "Now when Jesus was born in Bethlehem of Judaea in the days of Herod the king,

GIRLS: behold, there came wise men from the east to Jerusalem, saying,

BOYS: Where is he that is born King of the Jews?

ALL: for we have seen his star in the east, and are come to worship him.

GIRL 1: When Herod the king had heard these things, he was troubled, and all Jerusalem with him.

Boys: And when he had gathered all the chief priests and scribes of the people together, he demanded of them where Christ should be born.

Girls: And they said unto him, In Bethlehem of Judaea:

Girl 2: for thus it is written by the prophet,

Boy 2: And thou Bethlehem, in the land of Juda, art not the least among the princes of Juda: for out of thee shall come a Governor, that shall rule my people Israel.

Girl 1: Then Herod, when he had privily called the wise men, inquired of them diligently what time the star appeared.

Boy 1: And he sent them to Bethlehem, and said,

Boys: Go, and search diligently for the young child; and when you have found him, bring me word again, that I may come and worship him also.

Girl 2: When they had heard the king, they departed;

Girls: And, lo, the star, which they saw in the east, went before them,

All: Till it came and stood over where the young child was.

Boys: When they saw the star, they rejoiced with exceeding great joy. And when they were come into the house, they saw the young child

Girls: with Mary his mother, and fell down, and worshipped him:

Boy 1: and when they had opened their treasures,

Girl 1: they presented unto him gifts;

Boys: gold,

Girls: and frankincense,

ALL: and myrrh."

(*Dim out or turn off the overhead lights. Spotlight the* THREE KINGS. *The* SPEECH CHOIR *leaves the platform in the darkness. The light follows the* KINGS *as they move.* MARY *takes her place in the darkness. She sits on a bench or stool, holding the child.*)

THE THREE KINGS (*singing as they enter*): "We Three Kings of Orient Are"

(*Let them sing it in unison, unaccompanied. Work on the timing so that they reach the front of the auditorium by the time they finish the first stanza and chorus. One king sings stanza 2 as he moves to the platform, kneels before the mother and child, and offers his gift. The other two kings sing the chorus with him. Stanzas 3 and 4 are done by the other two kings in like manner. They rise and depart during stanza 5.*)

SPOTLIGHT: *Off of Nativity and upon the* STORYTELLER.

STORYTELLER: The kings brought Jesus the most costly products of the countries in which they lived. How appropriate! Gifts for a newborn King—a King who came into the world to GIVE—a King whose sacrificial giving led to a hill called Calvary.

Through the ages, followers of Christ the world around have reflected his spirit in giving. Such a one was Martin, a humble Russian shoemaker.

(*Tell the story "Where Love Is, There God Is Also," page 68.*)

PRAYER: THE PASTOR

(*During the prayer, the* STORYTELLER *quietly moves from the platform. The* SPOTLIGHT *picks up the* PASTOR *on the auditorium floor level. The prayer should lead into the climactic feature, the bringing of gifts to the front of the auditorium. Ask a* SOLOIST *to sing "What Can I Give to Jesus" just before or immediately after the gift sharing time.*)

STAGING DIRECTIONS

Speech Choir

"How-to Instructions" give techniques for the speech choir.

The Tableau

Elevate the tableau so all characters can be seen. Use a blanket wrapped around a bundle of cloth to represent the baby. "How-to Instructions" will help in creating tableaux.

Costuming, Make-up, Lighting, Scenery

See "How-to Instructions."

The White Gifts

Be sure to decide several weeks in advance what items are needed and to whom they'll be given. Share this information with the people. They'll need several reminders in regard to the white wrappings.

The Storyteller

The storyteller is vital to the program. Be sure to give him the story at least six weeks in advance of the presentation date. Cut and edit the story to meet the needs of your group.

WHERE LOVE IS, THERE GOD IS ALSO
Leo Tolstoi

Shoemaker Martyn Avdyeich lived in the city. He lived in a basement, in a room with one window. The window looked out on the street. Through it the people could be seen as they passed by: though only the feet were visible, Martyn Avdyeich could tell the men by their boots. He had lived for a long time in one place and had many acquaintances. It was a rare pair of boots in the neighborhood that had not gone once or twice through his hands. Some he had resoled; on others he had put patches, or fixed the seams, or even put on new uppers. Frequently he saw his own work through the window. He had much to do, for he did honest work, put in strong material, took no more than was fair, and kept his word. If he could get a piece of work done by a certain time he undertook to do it, and if not, he would not cheat, but said so in advance. Everybody knew Avdyeich, and his work never stopped.

Avdyeich had always been a good man, but in his old age he thought more of his soul and came near unto God. Even while Martyn had been living with a master, his wife had died, and he had been left with a boy three years of age. Their children did not live long. All the elder children had died before. At first Martyn had intended sending his son to his sister in a village, but then he felt sorry for the little lad, and thought: "It will be hard for my Kapitoshka to grow up in somebody else's family, and so I will keep him."

Avdyeich left his master, and took up quarters with his son. But God did not grant Avdyeich any luck with his children. No sooner had the boy grown up so as to be a help to his father and a joy to him, than a disease fell upon him and he lay down and had a fever for a week and died. Martyn buried his son, and was in despair. He despaired so much that he began to murmur against God. He was so downhearted that more than once he asked God to let him die, and rebuked God for having taken his beloved only son, and not him. He even stopped going to church.

One day an old man, a countryman of Avdyeich's, returning from Troitsa,—he had been a pilgrim for eight years—came to see him. Avdyeich talked with him and began to complain of his sorrow:

"I have even no desire to live any longer, godly man. If I could only die. That is all I am praying God for. I am a man without any hope."

And the old man said to him:

"You do not say well, Martyn. We cannot judge God's works. Not by our reason, but by God's judgment do we live. God has determined that your son should die, and you live. Evidently it is better so. The reason you are in despair is that you want to live for your own enjoyment."

"What else shall we live for?" asked Martyn.

And the old man said:

"We must live for God, Martyn. He gives us life, and for Him must we live. When you shall live for Him and shall not worry about anything, life will be lighter for you."

Martyn was silent, and he said:

"How shall we live for God?"

And the old man said:

"Christ has shown us how to live for God. Do you know how to read? If so, buy yourself a Gospel and read it, and you will learn from it how to live for God. It tells all about it."

These words fell deep into Avdyeich's heart. And he went that very day and bought himself a New Testament in large letters, and began to read.

Avdyeich had meant to read it on holidays only, but when he began to read it, his heart was so rejoiced that he read it every day. Many a time he buried himself so much in reading that all the kerosene would be spent in the lamp, but he could not tear himself away from the book. And Avdyeich read in it every morning, and the more he read, the clearer it became to him what God wanted of him, and how he should live for God; and his heart grew lighter and lighter. Formerly, when he lay down to sleep, he used to groan and sob and think of his Kapitoshka, but now he only muttered:

"Glory be to Thee, glory to Thee, O Lord! Thy will be done!"

Since then Avdyeich's life had been changed. Formerly, he used on a holiday to frequent the tavern, to drink tea, and would not decline a drink of vodka. He would drink a glass with an acquaintance and, though he would not be drunk, he would come out of the tavern in a happier mood, and then he would speak foolish things, and would scold, or slander a man. Now all that passed away from him. His life came to be calm and happy. In the morning he sat down to work, and when he got through, he took the lamp from the hook, put it down on the table, fetched the book from the shelf; opened it, and began to read it. And the more he read, the better he understood it, and his mind was clearer and his heart lighter.

One evening Martyn read late into the night. He had before him the Gospel of St. Luke. He read chapter six and the verses: "And unto him that smiteth thee on the one cheek offer also the other; and him that taketh away thy cloke forbid not to take thy coat also. Give to every man that asketh of thee; and of him that taketh away thy goods ask them not again. And as ye would that men should do to you, do ye also to them likewise."

And he read also the other verses, where the Lord says: "And why call ye me, Lord, Lord, and do not the things which I say? Whosoever cometh to me, and heareth my sayings, and doeth them, I will shew you to whom he is like: he is like a man which built an house, and digged deep, and laid the foundation on a rock: and when the flood arose, the stream beat vehemently upon that house, and could not shake it: for it was founded upon a rock. But he that heareth, and doeth not, is like a man that without a foundation built an house upon the earth; against which the stream did beat vehemently, and immediately it fell; and the ruin of that house was great."

When Avdyeich read these words, there was joy in his heart. He took off his glasses, put them on the book, leaned his arms on the table, and fell to musing. And he began to apply these words to his life, and he thought:

"Is my house on a rock, or on the sand? It is well if it is founded on a rock: it is so easy to sit alone,—it seems to me that I am doing everything which God has commanded; but if I dissipate, I shall sin again. I will just proceed as at present. It is so nice! Help me, God!"

This he thought, and he wanted to go to sleep, but he was loath to tear himself away from the book. And he began to read the seventh chapter. He read about the centurion, about the widow's son, about the answer to John's disciples, and he reached the passage where the rich Pharisee invited the Lord to be his guest, and where the sinning woman anointed His feet and washed them with her tears, and he justified her. And he reached the 44th verse, and read: "And he turned to the woman, and said unto Simon, Seest thou this woman? I entered into thine house, thou gavest me no water for my feet: but she hath washed my feet with tears, and wiped them with the hairs of her head. Thou gavest me no kiss: but this woman since the time I came in hath not ceased to kiss my feet. My head with oil thou didst not anoint: but this woman hath anointed my feet with ointment."

When he had read these verses, he thought:

"He gave no water for His feet; he gave no kiss; he did not anoint His head with oil."

And again Avdyeich took off his glasses and placed them on the book, and fell to musing.

"Evidently he was just such a Pharisee as I am. He, no doubt, thought only of himself: how to drink tea, and be warm, and in comfort, but he did not think of the guest. About himself he thought, but no care did he have for the guest. And who was the guest?—The Lord Himself. Would I have done so, if He had come to me?"

And Avdyeich leaned his head on both his arms and did not notice how he fell asleep.

"Martyn!" suddenly something seemed to breathe over his very ear.

Martyn shuddered in his sleep: "Who is that?"

He turned around and looked at the door, but there was nobody there. He bent down again, to go to sleep. Suddenly he heard distinctly:

"Martyn, oh, Martyn, remember, to-morrow I will come to the street."

Martyn awoke, rose from his chair, and began to rub his eyes. He did not know himself whether he had heard these words in his dream or in waking. He put out the light and went to sleep.

Avdyeich got up in the morning before daybreak, said his prayers, made a fire, put the beet soup and porridge on the stove, started the samovar, tied on his apron, and sat down at the window to work. And, as he sat there at work, he kept thinking of what had happened the night before. His thoughts were divided: now he thought that it had only seemed so to him, and now again he thought he had actually heard the voice.

"Well," he thought, "such things happen."

Martyn was sitting at the window and not so much working as looking out into the street, and if somebody passed in unfamiliar boots, he bent over to look out of the window, in order to see not merely the boots, but also the face. A janitor passed by in new felt boots; then a water-carrier went past; then an old soldier of the days of Nicholas, in patched old felt boots, holding a shovel in his hands, came in a line with the window. Avdyeich recognized him by his felt boots. The old man's name was Stepanych, and he was living with a neighboring merchant for charity's sake. It was his duty to help the janitor. Stepanych began to clear away the snow opposite Avdyeich's window. Avdyeich cast a glance at him and went back to work.

"Evidently I am losing my senses in my old age," Avdyeich laughed to himself. "Stepanych is clearing away the snow, and I thought that Christ was coming to see me. I, old fool, am losing my senses." But before he had made a dozen stitches, something drew him again toward the window. He looked out, and there he saw Stepanych leaning his shovel against the wall and either warming or resting himself.

He was an old, broken-down man, and evidently shoveling snow was above his strength. Avdyeich thought: "I ought to give him some tea; fortunately the samovar is just boiling." He stuck the awl into the wood, got up, placed the samovar on the table, put some tea in the teapot, and tapped with his finger at the window. Stepanych turned around and walked over to the window. Avdyeich beckoned to him and went to open the door.

"Come in and get warmed up!" he said. "I suppose you are feeling cold."

"Christ save you! I have a breaking in my bones," said Stepanych.

He came in, shook off the snow and wiped his boots so as not to track the floor, but he was tottering all the time.

"Don't take the trouble to rub your boots. I will clean up,—that is my business. Come and sit down!" said Avdyeich. "Here, drink a glass of tea!"

Avdyeich filled two glasses and moved one of them up to his guest, and himself poured his glass into the saucer and began to blow at it.

Stepanych drank his glass; then he turned it upside down, put the lump of sugar on top of it, and began to express his thanks; but it was evident that he wanted another glass.

"Have some more," said Avdyeich; and he poured out a glass for his guest and one for himself. Avdyeich drank his tea, but something kept drawing his attention to the window.

"Are you waiting for anybody?" asked the guest.

"Am I waiting for anybody? It is really a shame to say for whom I am waiting: no, I am not exactly waiting, but a certain word has fallen deep into my heart: I do not know myself whether it is a vision, or what. You see, my friend, I read the Gospel yesterday about Father Christ and how He suffered and walked the earth. I suppose you have heard of it?"

"Yes, I have," replied Stepanych, "but we are ignorant people, —we do not know how to read."

"Well, so I read about how He walked the earth. I read, you know, about how He came to the Pharisee, and the Pharisee did not give Him a good reception. Well, my friend, as I was reading last night about that very thing, I wondered how he could have failed to honor Father Christ. If He should have happened to come to me, for example, I should have done everything to receive Him. But he did not receive Him well. As I was thinking of it, I fell asleep. And as I dozed off I heard some one calling me by name: I got up and it was as though somebody were whispering to me: 'Wait,' he said: 'I will come tomorrow.' This he repeated twice. Would you believe it,—it has been running through my head,—I blame myself for it,— and I am, as it were, waiting for Father Christ."

Stepanych shook his head and said nothing. He finished his

glass and put it sidewise, but Avdyeich took it again and filled it with tea.

"Drink, and may it do you good! I suppose when He, the Father, walked the earth, He did not neglect anybody, and kept the company mostly of simple folk. He visited mostly simple folk, and chose His disciples mostly from people of our class, laboring men, like ourselves the sinners. He who raises himself up, He said, shall be humbled, and he who humbles himself shall be raised. You call me Lord, He said, but I will wash your feet. He who wants to be the first, He said, let him be everybody's servant; because, He said, blessed are the poor, the meek, the humble, and the merciful."

Stepanych forgot his tea. He was an old man and easily moved to tears. He sat there and listened, and tears flowed down his cheeks.

"Take another glass!" said Avdyeich.

But Stepanych made the sign of the cross, thanked him for the tea, pushed the glass away from him, and got up.

"Thank you, Martyn Avdyeich," he said. "You were hospitable to me, and have given food to my body and my soul."

"You are welcome. Come in again—I shall be glad to see you," said Avdyeich.

Stepanych went away. Martyn poured out the last tea, finished another glass, put away the dishes, and again sat down at the window to work,—to tap a boot. And as he worked, he kept looking out of the window,—waiting for Christ and thinking of Him and His works. And all kinds of Christ's speeches ran through his head.

There passed by two soldiers, one in Crown boots, the other in boots of his own; then the proprietor of a neighboring house came by in clean galoshes, and then a baker with a basket. All of these went past the window, and then a woman in woollen stockings and peasant shoes came in line with the window. She went by the window and stopped near a wall. Avdyeich looked at her through the window, and saw that she was a strange, poorly dressed woman, with a child: she had stopped with her back to the wind and was trying to wrap the child, though she did not have anything to wrap it in. The woman's clothes were for the summer, and scanty at that. Avdyeich could hear the child cry in the street, and her vain attempt to quiet it. Avdyeich got up and went out of his room and up to the staircase, and called out:

"Clever woman! Clever woman!"

The woman heard him and turned around.

"Why are you standing there in the cold with the child? Come in here! It will be easier for you to wrap the child in a warm room. Here, this way!"

The woman was surprised. She saw an old man in an apron, with glasses over his nose, calling to her. She followed him in.

They went down the stairs and entered the room, and Martyn took the woman up to the bed.

"Sit down here, clever woman, nearer to the stove, and get warm and feed the child."

"There is no milk in my breasts,—I have not had anything to eat since morning," said the woman, but still she took the child to her breast.

Avdyeich shook his head, went to the table, fetched some bread and a bowl, opened a door in the stove, filled the bowl with beet soup, and took out the pot of porridge, but it was not done yet. He put the soup on the table, put down the bread, and took off a rag from a hook and put it down on the table.

"Sit down, clever woman, and eat, and I will sit with the babe,—I used to have children of my own, and so I know how to take care of them."

The woman made the sign of the cross, sat down at the table, and began to eat, while Avdyeich seated himself on the bed with the child. He smacked his lips at it, but could not smack well, for he had no teeth. The babe kept crying all the time. Avdyeich tried to frighten it with his finger: he quickly carried his finger down toward the babe's mouth and pulled it away again. He did not put his finger into the child's mouth, because it was black,—all smeared with pitch. But the child took a fancy for his finger and grew quiet, and then even began to smile. Avdyeich, too, was happy. The woman was eating in the meantime and telling him who she was and whither she was going.

"I am a soldier's wife," she said. "My husband was driven somewhere far away eight months ago, and I do not know where he is. I had been working as a cook when the baby was born; they would not keep me with the child. This is the third month that I have been without a place. I have spent all I had saved. I wanted to hire out as a wet-nurse, but they will not take me: they say that I am too thin. I went to a merchant woman, where our granny lives, and she promised she would take me. I thought she wanted me to come at once, but she told me she wanted me next week. She lives a distance away. I am all worn out and have worn out the dear child, too. Luckily our landlady pities us for the sake of Christ, or else I do not know how we should have lived until now."

Avdyeich heaved a sigh, and said:

"And have you no warm clothes?"

"Indeed, it is time now to have warm clothing, dear man! But yesterday I pawned my last kerchief for twenty kopeks."

The woman went up to the bed and took her child, but Avdyeich got up, went to the wall, rummaged there awhile, and brought her an old sleeveless cloak.

"Take this!" he said. "It is an old piece, but you may use it to wrap yourself in."

The woman looked at the cloak and at the old man, and took the cloak, and burst out weeping. Avdyeich turned his face away; he crawled under the bed, pulled out a box, rummaged through it, and again sat down opposite the woman.

And the woman said:

"May Christ save you, grandfather! Evidently He sent me to your window. My child would have frozen to death. When I went out it was warm, but now it has turned dreadfully cold. It was He, our Father, who taught you to look through the window and have pity on me, sorrowful woman."

Avdyeich smiled, and said:

"It is He who has instructed me: clever woman, there was good reason why I looked through the window."

Martyn told the soldier woman about his dream, and how he had heard a voice promising him that the Lord would come to see him on that day.

"'Everything is possible," said the woman. She got up, threw the cloak over her, wrapped the child in it, and began to bow to Avdyeich and to thank him.

"Accept this, for the sake of Christ," said Avdyeich, giving her twenty kopeks, with which to redeem her kerchief.

The woman made the sign of the cross, and so did Avdyeich, and he saw the woman out.

She went away. Avdyeich ate some soup, put the things away, and sat down once more to work. He was working, but at the same time thinking of the window: whenever it grew dark there, he looked up to see who was passing. There went by acquaintances and strangers, and there was nothing peculiar.

Suddenly Avdyeich saw an old woman, a huckstress, stop opposite the very window. She was carrying a basket with apples. There were but few of them left—evidently she had sold all, and over her shoulder she carried a bag with chips. No doubt, she had picked them up at some new building, and was on her way home. The bag was evidently pulling hard on her shoulder; she wanted to shift it to her other shoulder, so she let the bag down on the flagstones, set the applebasket on a post, and began to shake down the chips. While she was doing that, a boy in a torn cap leaped out from somewhere, grasped an apple from the basket, and wanted to skip out, but the old woman saw him in time and turned around and grabbed the boy by the sleeve. The boy yanked and tried to get away, but the old woman held on to him with both her hands, knocked down his cap, and took hold of his hair. The boy cried, and the old woman scolded. Avdyeich did not have time to put away the awl. He threw it on the floor, jumped out of the room, stumbled on the staircase, and dropped his glasses. He ran out into the street. The old woman was pulling the boy's hair and scolding him. She wanted to take him to a policeman; the little fellow struggled and tried to deny what he had done:

"I did not take any, so why do you beat me? Let me go!"

Avdyeich tried to separate them. He took the boy's arm, and said:

"Let him go, granny, forgive him for Christ's sake!"

"I will forgive him in such a way that he will not forget until the new bath brooms are ripe. I will take the rascal to the police station!"

Avdyeich began to beg the old woman:

"Let him go, granny, he will not do it again. Let him go, for Christ's sake!"

The woman let go of him. The boy wanted to run, but Avdyeich held on to him.

"Beg the grandmother's forgiveness," he said. "Don't do that again,—I saw you take the apple."

The boy began to cry, and he asked her forgiveness.

"That's right. And now, take this apple!" Avdyeich took an apple from the basket and gave it to the boy. "I will pay for it, granny," he said to the old woman.

"You are spoiling these ragamuffins," said the old woman. "He ought to be rewarded in such a way that he should remember it for a week."

"Oh, granny, granny!" said Avdyeich. "That is according to our ways, but how is that according to God's ways? If he is to be whipped for an apple, what ought to be done with us?"

The old woman grew silent.

And Avdyeich told the old woman the parable of the lord who forgave his servant his whole large debt, after which the servant went and took his fellow servant who was his debtor by the throat. The old woman listened to him, and the boy stood and listened, too.

"God has commanded that we should forgive," said Avdyeich, "or else we, too, shall not be forgiven. All are to be forgiven, but most of all an unthinking person."

The old woman shook her head and sighed.

"That is so," said the old woman, "but they are very much spoiled nowadays."

"Then we old people ought to teach them," said Avdyeich.

"That is what I say," said the old woman. "I myself had seven of them,—but only one daughter is left now." And the old woman began to tell where and how she was living with her daughter, and how many grandchildren she had. "My strength is waning," she said, "but still I work. I am sorry for my grandchildren, and they are such nice children,—nobody else meets me the way they do. Aksyutka will not go to anybody from me. 'Granny, granny dear, darling!'" And the old woman melted with tenderness.

"Of course, he is but a child,—God be with him!" the old woman said about the boy.

She wanted to lift the bag on her shoulders, when the boy jumped up to her, and said:

"Let me carry it, granny! I am going that way."

The old woman shook her head and threw the bag on the boy's shoulders. They walked together down the street. The old woman had forgotten to ask Avdyeich to pay her for the apple. Avdyeich stood awhile, looking at them and hearing them talk as they walked along.

When they disappeared from sight, he returned to his room. He found his glasses on the staircase,—they were not broken,—and he picked up his awl and again sat down to work. He worked for awhile; he could not find the holes with the bristle, when he looked up and saw the lampman lighting the lamps.

"It is evidently time to strike a light," he thought, and he got up and fixed the lamp and hung it on the hook, and sat down again to work. He finished a boot: he turned it around and looked at it, and he saw that it was well done. He put down his tool, swept up the clippings, put away the bristles and the remnants and the awls, took the lamp and put it on the table, and fetched the Gospel from the shelf. He wanted to open the book where he had marked it the day before with a morocco clipping, but he opened it in another place. And just as he went to open the Gospel, he thought of his dream of the night before. And just as he thought of it, it appeared to him as though something were moving and stepping behind him. He looked around, and, indeed, it looked as though people were standing in the dark corner, but he could not make out who they were. And a voice whispered to him:

"Martyn, oh, Martyn, have you not recognized me?"

"Whom?" asked Avdyeich.

"Me," said the voice. "It is I."

And out of the dark corner came Stepanych, and he smiled and vanished like a cloud and was no more.

"And it is I," said a voice.

And out of the dark corner came the woman with the babe, and the woman smiled and the child laughed, and they, too, disappeared.

"And it is I," said a voice.

And out came the old woman and the boy with the apple, and both smiled and vanished.

And joy fell on Avdyeich's heart, and he made the sign of the cross, put on his glasses, and began to read the Gospel, there where he had opened it. And at the top of the page he read:

"I was an hungered, and ye gave me meat: I was thirsty, and ye gave me drink: I was a stranger, and ye took me in."

And at the bottom of the page he read:

"Inasmuch as ye have done it unto one of the least of these my brethren, ye have done it unto me." (Matt. xxv.)

"And Avdyeich understood that his dream had not deceived him, that the Saviour had really come to him on that day, and that he had received Him."[1]

[1] From *The World's Greatest Christmas Stories,* collected by Eric Posselt. Used by permission of Mrs. Posselt.

The Christmas Story

Luke's account of Jesus' birth told by a speech choir and a singing choir, and portrayed in seven simple tableaux (posed pictures).

CHARACTERS

MARY
JOSEPH
ANGEL
SHEPHERDS
SIMEON
VARIOUS *people on the road to Bethlehem*
SPEECH CHOIR *(eight to sixteen people)*
SINGING CHOIR *or smaller singing groups*

PRELUDE *(organ or piano; use trumpets if available)*: "O Come All Ye Faithful"

(*The* SPEECH CHOIR *and* SINGING GROUPS *take their places.*)

HYMN *(congregation)*: "Joy to the World"

PRAYER (*Lights are turned off during the prayer, leaving the auditorium in darkness.*) SPOTLIGHT: *On the* SPEECH CHOIR *at the close of the prayer.*

SPEECH CHOIR: "And it came to pass in those days, that there went out a decree from Caesar Augustus, that all the world should be taxed. (And this taxing was first made when

Cyrenius was governor of Syria.) And all went to be taxed, every one into his own city."

SPOTLIGHT: *Off* SPEECH CHOIR *and up on* SCENE 1: *a group of people of various ages posed as if on their way to be taxed.*

CHOIR: (*Stanza 1*) "*O Little Town of Bethlehem*" (*To be sung as the audience focuses on the posed picture.*)

SPOTLIGHT: *Off* SCENE 1 *and up on* SPEECH CHOIR.

SPEECH CHOIR: "And Joseph also went up from Galilee, out of the city of Nazareth, into Judea, unto the city of David, which is called Bethlehem; . . . to be taxed with Mary his espoused wife, being great with child."

SPOTLIGHT: *Off* SPEECH CHOIR *and up on* SCENE 2: JOSEPH *and* MARY *on their way to be taxed.* JOSEPH *is helping* MARY *along. She is weary from the journey.*

CHOIR: (*Stanza 2*) "*O Little Town of Bethlehem*" (*Sung as the audience focuses attention on the posed picture.*)

SPOTLIGHT: *Off* SCENE 2 *and up on* SPEECH CHOIR.

SPEECH CHOIR: "And so it was, that, while they were there, the days were accomplished that she should be delivered. And she brought forth her firstborn son, and wrapped him in swaddling clothes, and laid him in a manger; because there was no room for them in the inn."

SPOTLIGHT: *Off* SPEECH CHOIR *and up on* SCENE 3: *the Nativity scene with* JOSEPH, MARY, *and the* BABE *in the manger.*

CHOIR: "Away in a Manger" (*Sung as the audience focuses on the posed picture.*)

SPOTLIGHT: *Off* SCENE 3 *and up on* SPEECH CHOIR.

SPEECH CHOIR: "And there were in the same country shepherds abiding in the field, keeping watch over their flock by night. And, lo, the angel of the Lord came upon them, and the glory of the Lord shone round about them: and they were sore afraid."

SPOTLIGHT: *Off* SPEECH CHOIR *and up on* SCENE 4: *three shepherds grouped to suggest that they are frightened by the angel's message.*

CHOIR: "While Shepherds Watched Their Flocks" (*As the audience focuses on the posed picture.*)

SPOTLIGHT: *Off* SCENE 4 *and up on* SPEECH CHOIR.

SPEECH CHOIR: "And the angel said unto them, Fear not: for, behold, I bring you good tidings of great joy, which shall be to all people. For unto you is born this day in the city of David a Saviour, which is Christ the Lord. And this shall be a sign unto you; Ye shall find the babe wrapped in swaddling clothes, lying in a manger. And suddenly there was with the angel a multitude of the heavenly host praising God, and saying, Glory to God in the highest, and on earth peace, good will toward men. And it came to pass, as the angels were gone away from them into heaven, the shepherds said one to another, Let us now go even unto Bethlehem, and see this thing which is come to pass, which the Lord hath made known unto us. And they came with haste, and found Mary, and Joseph, and the babe lying in a manger."

SPOTLIGHT: *Off* SPEECH CHOIR *and up on* SCENE 5: *the nativity scene with shepherds added.*

MUSIC: "Silent Night, Holy Night" (*Sung or played while audience focuses attention on the posed picture.*)

SPOTLIGHT: *Off* SCENE 5 *and up on* SPEECH CHOIR.

SPEECH CHOIR: "And when they had seen it, they made known abroad the saying which was told them concerning this child. And all they that heard it wondered at those things which were told them by the shepherds. But Mary kept all these things, and pondered them in her heart."

SPOTLIGHT: *Off* SPEECH CHOIR *and up on* SCENE 6: MARY *seated by the manger with a bundle in her arms, suggesting a baby.*

CHOIR: "Gentle Mary Laid Her Child"

SPOTLIGHT: *Off* SCENE 6 *and up on* SPEECH CHOIR.

SPEECH CHOIR: "And when eight days were accomplished for the circumcising of the child, his name was called JESUS, which was so named of the angel before he was conceived in the womb. And when the days of her purification according to the law of Moses were accomplished, they brought him to Jerusalem, to present him to the Lord. . . . And, behold, there was a devout man in Jerusalem, whose name was Simeon. . . . And it was revealed unto him by the Holy Ghost, that he should not see death, before he had seen the Lord's Christ. And he came by the Spirit into the temple: and when the parents brought in the child Jesus, . . . [Simeon] took him up in his arms, and blessed God, and said, Lord, now lettest thou thy servant depart in peace, according to thy word: For mine eyes have seen my salvation, which thou hast prepared before the face of all people; a light to lighten the Gentiles, and the glory of thy people Israel."

SPOTLIGHT: *Off* SPEECH CHOIR *and up on* SCENE 7: *the old man,* SIMEON, *holding the Christ child.*

CHOIR: (*Stanza 4*) "It Came Upon the Midnight Clear" (*Sung as the audience focuses on the posed picture.*)

Prayer: (*Led by* PASTOR)

SPOTLIGHT: *Off* SCENE 7 *during prayer; house lights are turned on.*

The Christmas Story

Staging Directions

Speech Choir

A speech choir to tell the story will add an exciting dimension to the program. This is another good way to use more people. Sixteen to twenty individuals can easily be used in a speech choir. Variety can be achieved by using two speech choirs. One may be composed of older children and the other youth or adults.

Several hours of preparation will be necessary, so be sure to get it going at least six weeks before the presentation.

Use "How-to Instructions" for the speech choir.

Platform Arrangement

Make use of every possible area in the auditorium including the baptistry, choir space, platform, steps leading up to the platform, a balcony, and the floor level of the auditorium.

Elevate the speech choir and tableaux so that they can be seen from every angle in the auditorium. People in the audience *must* be able to see what's happening at all times.

Place the speech choir as far away from the tableau areas as possible. The tableau scenes will be formed in the darkness while the spotlight is focused on the speech choir. Keep the people in the speech choir as close together as possible so they can all hear each other.

Seat the singing groups in the auditorium. They will sing in the darkness while attention is focused on the tableaux.

Arranging the Tableaux

Use "How-to Instructions" in creating tableaux.

Costuming, Make-up, Lighting, Scenery

Consult "How-to Instructions."

Christmas Eve Family Worship

Prelude—Appropriate Christmas Recording

Responsive Reading:

FATHER (*or* LEADER): "And it came to pass in those days, that there went out a decree from Caesar Augustus, that all the world should be taxed."

FAMILY: "And Joseph also went up from Galilee, out of the city of Nazareth, into Judea, unto the city of David, which is called Bethlehem; (because he was of the house and lineage of David:)"

FATHER: "To be taxed with Mary his espoused wife, being great with child."

FAMILY: "And so it was, that while they were there, the days were accomplished that she should be delivered."

FATHER: "And she brought forth her firstborn son, and wrapped him in swaddling clothes, and laid him in a manger; because there was no room for them in the inn."

PRAYER (MOTHER *or other* FAMILY MEMBER):

HYMN: "Silent Night"
Silent night, Holy night, All is calm
all is bright

Round yon Virgin Mother and child!
  Holy Infant so tender and mild,
Sleep in heavenly peace, Sleep in
  heavenly peace.

Silent night, Holy night, Wondrous Star,
  lend thy light;
With the angels let us sing, Alleluia to
  our King;
Christ the Saviour is born, Christ the
  Saviour is born.

The Christmas Story from the Bible:

Luke 2:8-14.
"And there were in the same country shepherds abiding in the field, keeping watch over their flock by night.

And lo, the angel of the Lord came upon them, and the glory of the Lord shone round about them: and they were sore afraid.

And the angel said unto them, Fear not: for, behold, I bring you good tidings of great joy which shall be to all people.

For unto you is born this day in the city of David a Saviour, which is Christ the Lord.

And this shall be a sign unto you: Ye shall find the babe wrapped in swaddling clothes, lying in a manger.

And suddenly there was with the angel a multitude of the heavenly host praising God, and saying,

Glory to God in the highest, and on earth peace, good will toward men."

Family Christmas Story: Was It True?

The story is told about the shepherd of Christmas who saw but did not follow the star. Decades later he held a grandson on his knee. He told the stirring story of that night.

When he finished the boy said: "Is that all? What did you do when you heard the good news? Was it true? Was the Christ child really born?"

The old man shook a pathetic snowy white head and answered: "I never knew. Some say it was true; some say it was all a myth. I did not take the trouble to go and see."

Luke 2:15 and 16.

"And it came to pass, as the angels were gone away from them into heaven, the shepherds said one to another, Let us now go even unto Bethlehem, and see this thing which is come to pass, which the Lord hath made known unto us. And they came with haste, and found Mary, and Joseph, and the babe lying in a manger."

Family prayers of thanks for the coming of Christ.

Join hands in a fellowship circle and give each family member an opportunity to pray.

This program is used by permission of D. K. Harrell, First Baptist Church, West Palm Beach, Florida.

The Inn That Missed Its Chance

This brief piece is appropriate for use as the final feature of the annual Christmas program. It can also be used in opening assemblies.

(*The* STRANGER *and the* INNKEEPER *enter. The* INNKEEPER *moves to the left side of the platform, stage left, and freezes, back to the audience. The* STRANGER *simultaneously comes to the front, center of the platform and speaks directly to the audience.*)

STRANGER: It was not my good fortune to be in Bethlehem that night—the night of his birth. But I have seen Jesus on two occasions recently.

One day, I stood and listened to him teach—such teaching I have never before heard. The other time I saw him was at the home of Mary and Martha. Yes, I saw it with my own eyes—I saw Jesus raise Lazarus from the dead—when he had been in the grave for four days!

These past days, my thoughts have been filled with the strange but wonderful teachings of Jesus. I do not know how or when it happened, but there came over me an impelling desire to visit the place of his birth—to see for myself the little village, the inn, the stable—and to—perhaps talk with the innkeeper.

I went to Bethlehem. I found the innkeeper. We talked. (*The* STRANGER *moves to the area where the* INNKEEPER *is*

standing. The INNKEEPER *turns toward the audience, bows to the* STRANGER *and points him to a chair. The* STRANGER *sits. They converse.*)

INNKEEPER: They tell me you've seen Him—witnessed His miracles.

STRANGER: Yes, it is true.

INNKEEPER: And you wish to know from me the events of that—that strange night. Well—well—

"What could be done? The inn was full of folks:
His honor, Marcus Lucius, and his scribes
Who made the census; honorable men
From farthest Galilee, come hitherward
To be enrolled; high ladies and their lords;
The rich, the rabbis, such a noble throng
As Bethlehem had never seen before
And may not see again. And there they were,
Close-herded with their servants, till the inn
Was like a hive at swarming-time, and I
Was fairly crazed among them.

"Could I know
That *they* were so *important? Just the two,*
No servants, just a workman sort of man,
Leading a donkey, and his wife thereon
Drooping and pale,—I saw them not myself,
My servants must have driven them away;
But had I seen them,—how was I to know?
Were inns to welcome stragglers, up and down
In all our towns from Beersheba to Dan,
Till He should come? And how were men to know?
There was a sign, they say, a heavenly light
Resplendent: but I had no time for stars,
And there were songs of angels in the air

Out on the hills; but how was I to hear
Amid the thousand clamors of an inn?

"Of course, if I had known them, who they were,
And who was He that should be born that night—
For now I learn that they will make him King,
A second David, who will ransom us
From these Philistine Romans—who but he
That feeds an army with a loaf of bread,
And if a soldier falls, he touches him
And up he leaps, uninjured?—Had I known,
I would have turned the whole inn upside down,
His honor, Marcus Lucius, and the rest,
And sent them all to stables.

"So you have seen him, stranger, and perhaps
Again may see him? Prithee say for me
I did not know; and if he comes again,
As he will surely come, with retinue,
And banners, and an army—tell him my Lord
That all my inn is his to make amends."

STRANGER (*rising*): Yes, I will see Him again—I *must* see Him again—and I will carry your message to Him.

(*He exits. The* INNKEEPER *watches him go and then speaks.*)

INNKEEPER: "Alas, alas! to miss a chance like that!
This inn that might be chief among them all—
The birthplace of the Messiah,—had I known!"[1]

(*He freezes for two or three seconds and exits.*)

STAGING DIRECTIONS

Platform Arrangement

A couple chairs or a bench will easily suggest the inn.

[1] Reprinted from *The Christian Endeavor World*. Used by permission.

The piece can be effectively done with all overhead lights on and without a spotlight.

It can be presented in contemporary clothing or in biblical costume. If biblical costumes are used, see "How-to Instructions." Makeup instructions can be found there also.

Jesus, the Savior

This program takes us to the manger and far beyond to the crucifixion. In three monologues, we get a glimpse of Christ, the Savior as seen through the eyes of the Woman at the Well, the Apostle Paul, and John the beloved Disciple.

A Suggested Order of Service

PRELUDE: Medley of Christmas hymns

PROCESSIONAL CAROL: "O Come, All Ye Faithful"

PRAYER

CAROL: "Silent Night"

THE BIRTH OF JESUS FORETOLD
 READER—Isaiah 9:6–7
 CAROL—"Angels, from the Realms of Glory"

THE ANNOUNCEMENT TO MARY
 READER—Luke 1:26–38
 CAROL—"Hark, the Herald Angels Sing"

MARY'S SONG OF THANKSGIVING
 READER—Luke 1:46–55
 CAROL—"It Came Upon the Midnight Clear"

THE BIRTH OF JESUS
 READER—Luke 2:1–7
 CHOIR—"Gentle Mary Laid Her Child"

Jesus, the Savior
: A dramatic presentation

Prayer Time

Hymn of Commitment

Benediction

The Dramatic Presentation

(*Leave all house lights on during the first part of the service. Dim out or turn off all lights at the close of the carol, "It Came Upon the Midnight Clear." Simultaneously focus spotlight on the* Reader.)

Reader: "And it came to pass in those days, that there went out a decree from Caesar Augustus, that all the world should be taxed. (And this taxing was first made when Cyrenius was governor of Syria.) And all went to be taxed, every one into his own city. And Joseph also went up from Galilee, out of the city of Nazareth, into Judea, unto the city of David, which is called Bethlehem; . . . to be taxed with Mary his espoused wife, being great with child. And so it was, that while they were there, the days were accomplished that she should be delivered. And she brought forth her firstborn son, and wrapped him in swaddling clothes, and laid him in a manger; because there was no room for them in the inn."

(Mary *and* Joseph *quietly slip into place and pose in the darkness while the* Reader *does the foregoing Scripture.*)

Spotlight: *Off of regular* Reader *and upon the manger scene.*

Choir: "Gentle Mary Laid Her Child" (*stanza 1*)

Spotlight: *Off of manger scene and upon the* Reader.

Reader: "Such a Babe in such a place,
　　Can He be the Saviour?

> Ask the saved of all the race
> Who have found His favor."[1]
> Ask Saul of Tarsus!
>
> (SAUL of TARSUS *slips into place in the darkness during the foregoing reading.*)

SPOTLIGHT: *Off of the* READER *and upon* SAUL *of* TARSUS.

MONOLOGUE: SAUL OF TARSUS
   (*During the closing lines of the monologue, the* SHEPHERDS *join the manger scene.*)

SPOTLIGHT: *Off of* SAUL *of* TARSUS *and upon* MANGER SCENE *with shepherds added.*

CHOIR: "Gentle Mary Laid Her Child" (*Repeat stanza 1*)

SPOTLIGHT: *Off of* MANGER SCENE *and upon the* READER.

READER: "Such a Babe in such a place,
   Can He be the Saviour?
   Ask the saved of all the race
   Who have found His favor."
   Ask the Woman at the Well.

(*The* WOMAN *at the* WELL *has moved into place during the foregoing narrative.*)

SPOTLIGHT: *Off of the* READER *and upon the* WOMAN *at the* WELL.

MONOLOGUE: *The Woman at the Well*
   (*The* SHEPHERDS *and* JOSEPH *exit, taking the manger with them.* MARY *sits on a stool or bench holding the baby. Use a bundle of cloth wrapped in a blanket. The* WISE MEN *join this scene and kneel before* MARY *and the Christ Child.*)

---

[1] From the hymn, "Gentle Mary Laid Her Child." Used by permission of Alta Lind Cook.

SPOTLIGHT: *Off of the* WOMAN *at the* WELL *and upon* MARY, JESUS, *and the* WISE MEN.

CHOIR: "Gentle Mary Laid Her Child" (*The first two lines of stanza 2 and the last 2 lines of stanza 1*)

SPOTLIGHT: *Off of the* TABLEAU *and upon the* READER.

READER: "Such a Babe in such a place,
Can He be the Saviour?
Ask the saved of all the race
Who have found His favor."
Ask John, the beloved disciple!

(*John gets into place during the* READER's *foregoing lines.*)

SPOTLIGHT: *Off the* READER *and upon* JOHN.

MONOLOGUE: *John, the Beloved*
(MARY *and the* WISE MEN *exit during the monologue. The* READER *sits.*)

SPOTLIGHT: *Off of* JOHN *and upon the* PASTOR OR LEADER *standing where the reader has been.*

PASTOR: "Such a Babe in such a place,
Can He be the Saviour?"
Yes, He can be—He is!

(*With houselights still off, give a brief testimony of your personal experience in Christ. Lead into the prayer time and hymn of commitment.*)

SAUL OF TARSUS[2]

I am a Jew, born in Tarsus. I was educated in Jerusalem under Gamaliel at whose feet I learned to follow our Jewish laws and customs very carefully.

---

[2] Three monologues adapted from *Living Gospels*, Kenneth N. Taylor, ed. (Wheaton, Ill.: Tyndale House, Publishers). Used by permission.

I used to believe that I ought to do many horrible things to the followers of Jesus of Nazareth. I breathed out threatenings and slaughter against the disciples of the Lord. I made havoc of the church. I imprisoned many of the saints in Jerusalem, as authorized by the High Priests; and when they were condemned to death, I cast my vote against them.

I persecuted Christians unto the death, both men and women. I used torture to try to make Christians everywhere curse Christ. I was so violently opposed to them that I even hounded them in distant cities in foreign lands.

I was on such a mission to Damascus, armed with the authority and commission of the chief priests, when one day about noon, a light from heaven brighter than the sun shone down on me and my companions.

We all fell down, and I heard a voice speaking to me in Hebrew,

"Saul, Saul, Why are you persecuting me?"

"Who are you?" I asked.

And the Lord replied, "I am Jesus, the one you are persecuting. Now stand up! For I have appeared to you to appoint you as My servant and My witness. You are to tell the world about this experience and about the many other occasions when I shall appear to you.

"And I will protect you from both your own people and the Gentiles. Yes, I am going to send you to the Gentiles. To open their eyes to their true condition so that they may repent and live in the light of God instead of in Satan's darkness."

I was not disobedient to that vision from heaven!

I preached first to those in Damascus, then in Jerusalem and through Judea, and also to the Gentiles that all must forsake their sins and turn to God.

The Jews arrested me in the temple for preaching this and tried to kill me.

I have been bound, beaten, stoned. I have been imprisoned, and I am ready not to be imprisoned only, but also to die for the name of the Lord Jesus.

THE WOMAN AT THE WELL

It seems strange that I should be the first one in our village to meet him. I saw him sitting there on the well that day as I approached with my water jar. As I drew near, he asked me for a drink. I was surprised that a Jew would ask a "despised Samaritan" for anything (usually they didn't even speak to us!) and I said, How is it that you, a Jew, ask me for a drink? I am a woman of Samaria and the Jews have no dealings with the Samaritans. He said, "If you only knew what a wonderful gift God has for you, and who I am, You would ask me for some *living water!*"

"But you don't have a rope or a bucket," I said, "and this is a very deep well! From where would you get this living water? And besides, are you greater than our ancestor Jacob? How can you offer better water than this which he and his sons and cattle enjoyed?"

He said, "People soon become thirsty again after drinking that water. But the water I give them, becomes a perpetual spring within them, watering them forever with eternal life."

"Please, sir," I said, "give me some of that water! Then I'll never be thirsty again and won't have to make this long trip out here every day."

Then he looked me straight in the eyes and said, "Go and get your husband."

"But I'm not married," I replied.

"All too true!" he said. "For you have had five husbands, and you aren't even married to the man you're living with now! You couldn't have spoken a truer word."

I had never in my life seen this man before. How could he know all this about *me*?

"Sir," I said, "You must be a prophet! But say, tell me, why is it that you Jews insist that Jerusalem is the only place of worship, while we Samaritans claim it is here, where our ancestors worshiped?"

Jesus, the Savior

He replied, "The time is coming, Ma'am, when we will no longer be concerned about whether to worship the Father here or in Jerusalem! For it's not *where* we worship that counts, but *how* we worship—is our worship spiritual and real?"

I said, "Well, at least I know that the Messiah will come—the one they call Christ—and when He does, He will explain everything to us."

Then, with a gentleness and tenderness I had never seen before, the stranger said, "I am the Messiah!"

Such news! I left my waterpot beside the well and ran back to the village. I told everyone, "Come and meet a man who told me everything I ever did! Can this be the Messiah?"

The people came streaming from the village to see him. And when they saw him at the well, they begged him to stay with us; and he did for two days. He taught us, and many others believed!

Then they said to me, "Now we believe because we have heard Him ourselves, not just because of what you told us. He is indeed the Savior of the World."

He stayed with us only two days—two days and our little village was never the same. We were thirsty—and He *quenched* our thirst with Living Water. He gave us a perpetual Spring and from that Spring within me, continues to flow rivers of Living Water!

JOHN, THE BELOVED DISCIPLE

I followed him that day when he called us from our fishing nets beside the Sea of Galilee. I was one of the twelve—the one closest to him during those brief years.

I was with him on that last dreadful day. Yes, I saw it all—

They stripped him, and put on him a scarlet robe. And when they had platted a crown of thorns, they put it upon his head, and a reed in his right hand: And they bowed the knee before him, and mocked him, saying, Hail, King of the Jews! And they spit upon him, and took the reed, and smote him on the head.

And when they were come to the place, which is called Calvary, there they crucified him.

He hung there in silent anguish, and they that passed by reviled him, wagging their heads, and saying, "If thou be the Son of God, come down from the cross!"

Beside me—watching sorrowfully—were his mother, and his mother's sister, Mary, the wife of Cleophas, and Mary Magdalene. When Jesus saw his mother standing near me, he said, "Woman, behold thy Son!" Then looking at me, he said, "Behold thy mother!" And from that hour I took her unto my own home.

Now from the sixth hour there was darkness over all the land unto the ninth hour. Then Jesus cried out in a loud voice, and said, "It is finished: and he bowed his head, and gave up the ghost." And, behold, the veil of the temple was rent in twain from the top to the bottom; and the earth did quake, and the rocks rent; and the graves were opened; and many bodies of the saints which slept arose, and came out of the graves. And the Centurion, standing by the cross, when he saw the earthquake, and the things that were done, said, "Truly, this was the Son of God."

Yes, I was there. I saw it happen. They nailed him to the cross—but they could not kill him! The grave could not contain him! He came forth—triumphant over death! I've seen him with my own eyes! I have touched him with my own hands! He is my Lord, my Savior! He is alive forevermore!

Staging Directions

Platform Arrangement

If possible, remove the lectern and all pulpit furniture from the platform for the entire service. Arrange the manger scenes on the left side of the platform and the monologues on the opposite side. Position these two playing areas as far apart as possible for the best lighting effects and so that each upcoming scene can be arranged in the darkness while the spotlight is focused on another area. Be sure that the scenes are elevated sufficiently for people to see. Remember, those who sit behind someone have to look over shoulders, etc. Look around and find sturdy tables and other levels that can be used.

Let the reader work from the floor level, standing behind a small speaker stand, just in front of the pulpit area. He can sit on the front pew while the monologues are being done.

Seat the choir with the congregation, placing them near the front.

The Monologues

Youth or adults should be chosen for the monologues. Seek out individuals who are imaginative and animated—the kind of people who can feel something deeply and can communicate their feelings to an audience. The individuals who are chosen must be able to memorize.

At least six weeks in advance of the presentation, bring together the ones who have been chosen to do the monologues. Give out the scripts, and talk about what is involved. Challenge them with the exciting opportunity that is theirs.

Share with them the "How-to Instructions." Schedule specific times to work with each individual.

The Reader

Choose a good reader and put in his hands the "How-to Instructions."

Schedule several rehearsals with the reader prior to the final rehearsals.

The Tableaux

Use "How-to Instructions" in arranging tableaux.

Rehearsals

Most of the rehearsing of the monologues can be done individually. At times when all of them are able to work together, they can help and encourage each other. Let one of them read a part of his monologue, putting as much feeling in it as possible. When he has finished, ask those who listened to share helpful suggestions.

How can he improve? Talk it over. Be honest with each other. After all have freely shared, repeat the process with another person reading.

Set a definite date at which time the monologues are to be memorized.

Schedule at least two full rehearsals with the reader, the monologues, tableaux, music, lights, costumes, and make-up. Be sure to rehearse with the sound system if one is to be used. The first essential in any program is that it be *heard*.

Costuming, Make-up, Lighting, Scenery

Use "How-to Instructions" for information.

How-to Instructions

Speech Choir

Choral speaking is an exciting means of communication whereby several voices (a speech choir) interpret a message to an audience. The cheering section at a football game is really nothing more than a huge speech choir directed by a few cheerleaders.

Choral speaking will add a touch of freshness to a program and is sure to catch and hold attention. It will require several hours of preparation, so be sure to get it going at least six weeks before the presentation.

Enlist one of your keenest people to work with the choral speaking group. This should be a person who is animated and dramatically inclined. Suggest that the group work out their own rehearsal schedule and meet two times a week.

Here are some basic steps that will help the inexperienced director:

1. Begin with a jingle such as "Peter Piper picked a peck of pickled peppers." Lead them in saying it until they are able to

>   BEGIN together

>   SPEAK at the same rate of speed

>   FINISH at the same split second

Make it fun! Help them loosen up and enjoy working together.

2. When togetherness has been established, begin work on

the Scripture to be interpreted. Take the first few lines and study them. Let different individuals read it as they think it should be done. Democratically choose the interpretation the group prefers. Let the individual whose reading was chosen do it again while the group listens. Talk about it. What words were given special emphasis? Where were the pauses? Where did the tempo speed up or slow down? What can we do to improve it?

When all are satisfied with the interpretation, do it together several times, with each person trying to blend his voice in with all the others.

Ask each person to mark his script, underscoring important words, indicating pauses, etc. This will help all to remember from one rehearsal to the next what was done.

3. No two directors use the same physical movement in directing. Many directors mark the strong beats in a line with a movement of the hand. Pitch may be indicated by the varying heights of the hand. Tempo may be indicated by the rapidity of hand movement.

4. It is the responsibility of the director to avoid the pitfall of a sing-song, dull, monotonous reading, a kind of chanting without meaning.

5. Does the director direct during a performance? If he does, he should be seated on the front row of the auditorium or in some other place where he will not be noticed. For the director to be seen directing is distracting and undesirable.

The aim should be a presentation in which the group is so prepared that they need no assistance from the director. Only then will their voices and faces come alive in an animated presentation.

A signal for beginning can be given by a member of the group without the audience ever being aware of it. It can be as simple as a quietly whispered "one" from someone near the center of the group.

6. The aim of the speech choir is unity. They should seem as one powerful voice, rather than a group of individuals.

Work for unity in thought, unity of feeling, unity in attack (all beginning at the exact same time), unity of articulation, and unity of pitch.

Spotlight

An effective follow spot can be improvised by use of a slide projector. Cut heavy cardboard in two inch squares. Take them to a printing company or book binder who has drills of various sizes. Get a different size hole punched in each card. The circle of light you get will be determined by the size of the hole and the distance between the slide projector and the scene you are lighting. A strip of gelatin held in front of the projector or taped on the cardboard slide will give the color you desire. See page 112 for source of gelatin.

The slide projector can be operated most effectively from a balcony. If worked from the back of the auditorium, it will need to be elevated so that it projects over the heads of the people in the congregation.

Scenery and Props

It is wise to use a minimum of scenery and props in the church auditorium. The audience can, in their imagination, supply the sheep which are grazing in the distance. They can also furnish the baby Jesus to go in the manger without seeing a big doll. A baby blanket made into a bundle will say it, or perhaps a light coming from within a deep manger will give the right atmosphere. Remember, the church auditorium is a place of worship and should not be cluttered with theatrical trappings. The audience can imaginatively construct better scenery than can be created in the church. We do not try to be realistic, but simply give enough help to fire the imagination of the audience. Working with minimum scenery and props in the place of worship will be in good taste.

Costuming

If carefully done, costumes can add beauty and authenticity

to a presentation. Why not set up a committee to do the costuming? This is a good way to use more people. Here are some suggestions to get them going.

1. Do some research so that the costumes will be authentic. Sunday School teaching pictures offer many ideas.
2. Think in terms of each tableau (posed picture). Seek to make each one excitingly different from the others.
3. Do a rough sketch of each costume, indicating the colors to be used and the type of headpiece.
4. For the inexperienced person, it is wise to do a "trial run." This can be done by making the costume from an old bed sheet or some other scrap material. Dress someone in the finished costume. Look at it critically. What improvements are needed?
5. Be sure to make the hems in the tunics several inches wide. This will make it possible to use the costumes in future programs with people of various heights.
6. In creating the costumes, work for variety so that no two characters look the same. This can be achieved by style of costume, color, and type of headpiece. No two headpieces should look the same.
7. Help will be needed from the costume committee in dress rehearsals and for the presentation. It will be their job to adjust headpieces and sashes, and to see that each character is properly costumed.

Arranging Tableaux

A tableau is simply a representation of a scene by a person or group posed in costume.

Much of the success of a dramatic presentation depends upon what the audience sees. A play is actually a series of meaningful pictures, all of which tell a story. Are the pictures clear as to what they are supposed to say? Or does the audience have difficulty in figuring them out? The first glance at the shepherds should tell that they are frightened at the angel's appearance and his strange message. How can this be achieved? Talk it over with the people who make up each tableau (posed picture). Lead them to do some thinking as to who they are, what kind of people they are, why they are in the story, and what it would be like to experience such a thing in real life.

After doing this thinking, ask them to get into the position that they feel they would take under the circumstances of their particular scene. Look at their positions. Can they be seen? Are there different levels (one standing, one kneeling, etc.)? Does the picture communicate the message intended? Is it meaningful? Does it depict emotion? Rearrange the picture, if necessary, to achieve your desired result.

Ask the entire cast to criticize the tableau. Let them show what they would do with the picture by rearranging the people in the scene. In this way the entire group may be kept interested. Their suggestions will be helpful.

Much time can be saved if in the first rehearsal you work separately with each tableau group. Then put the tableaux, music, and other elements all together in final rehearsals!

Make-up

Very little make-up is needed in the church. Use just enough to offset the artificial light and to make the characters look like real people.

Biblical plays usually call for a few beards. The only way to learn how to put on a beard is to practice doing it. Crepe hair, which comes in a variety of colors, is the main ingredient used in making a beard. Liquid latex is the best adhesive to fasten the crepe hair to the face. This material is similar to rubber cement and can easily be peeled off without any irritation or harm to the skin.

Get the material (see page 112 for source of make-up materials), read the directions, experiment with it. Make a beard. Look at it. Does it look real? If not, why not? Take it off and make another one. This is fun and very rewarding.

When sufficient skill has been gained, start making the beards to be used in the presentation. If each beard has a good liquid latex base (three or four layers) it can be carefully peeled off and used over and over. This means that the beards can be made in advance of the program at the convenience of the make-up committee and those needing beards. With a little bit of latex, the beards can be fastened back on in a matter of a few minutes.

Monologues

This simple form of drama appeals to all ages. One person speaks alone and, for the moment, shares the thoughts and feelings of the character being portrayed.

These simple steps in preparation will help the inexperienced director:

1. Study all available background material on the character to be portrayed. Get to "know" him as intimately as possible. Ask yourself questions such as these: How old is he? What was his background? What does he say about himself? What does he say about others? What does he *do*?

2. Lead the person who is to do the monologue to do likewise.

3. Then discuss with him the character. Talk it out. Lead him to discover the central idea that is to be communicated (the message).

4. Motivate him to think creatively. You must fire his imagination! Otherwise, he will be unexcited about what he is doing. He may even be dull!

5. Lead him to do his own creating with motivation and guidance from you.

6. The central aim of the person doing the monologue should be to "live the part"—to imaginatively *become* the person he is seeking to portray. When this happens, the message comes through with honesty and believability and the audience is invariably moved!

7. Work far enough ahead that a memorized presentation will be possible. Only then will the monologue totally come to life.

8. Decide whether or not a special costume will be needed. Remember, even a biblical monologue can be done effectively in contemporary dress.

Creative Reading

Each program in this book has a Scripture passage as its background. It is vital that these Scriptures be read with excitement and animation. Too often, they are done in a dull, lifeless manner, inviting boredom and lack of attention on the part of the would-be hearers.

These simple suggestions for readers can make the ink on the page come alive:

1. Your chief aim as a reader is to convey a message. You must catch attention, hold attention, and present your thoughts and feelings so convincingly that the audience will respond.

2. Imagination is the key! Without it, the voice is hard and neutral.

3. The first step in creative reading is to find the meaning of the author. Make a thorough study of the material to be read. Look at it sentence by sentence, and word by word. Look up words that are vague in meaning or in any way strange to you. It is impossible to communicate to another that which you yourself do not clearly understand.

Mark words that deserve special emphasis.

4. After discovering the thought the author has in mind, you must *think that thought* as you speak it. If you do, you are very likely to convey the right meaning.

Too many readers read "words, words, words," instead of thought and ideas. This makes the reading artificial, monotonous, stumbling, and unconvincing.

5. Work for honesty and sincerity. The average person reads more poorly than he speaks. His speech is usually direct, sincere, unaffected, spontaneous, interesting, and convincing because he thinks of speech as a means of communicating ideas.

6. At the very moment you are speaking the author's words, imagine that you are experiencing with your senses the move-

ments suggested by the words.

As you read, create in the imagination the sight images suggested by the words. In rehearsing, lift your eyes from the book and picture on the back wall of the room the mental image the words convey. Do not allow yourself to speak a phrase until you have created the mental picture suggested by the phrase. Do not rush. Take all the time you need to get the thought from the words and to create the mental picture with your eyes off the script. Concentrate on the mental picture as you read. Remember, *impression* comes before *expression.*

7. The more profound the thought you are expressing, the longer and more frequent the pause. The pause may be used just before a single word, or just after a single word to point up that word. The pause may come after a phrase, as a clause, or a complete sentence.

Sometimes the pause is indicated with punctuation, but most of the time the reader must sense the need to pause even without punctuation to guide him.

A pause is not a stop in the sense of finality. Instead, it is a silence wherein the idea continues, a silence used to impress the importance of words just spoken or about to be spoken.

When pauses are used effectively, both reader and audience are unconscious of the length of the pause. Their attention is focused upon the author's meaning and not upon the period of silence.

8. Spontaneity can best be achieved through a process called "The Illusion of the First Time." You simply try to react to each idea with such freshness of appreciation that you give the illusion that the significance of the idea just flashed upon you at the moment of delivery.

9. Don't think of *how* you're reading. Respond to the author's idea. Respond honestly, with sincere emotion. True emotional response on your part will color your words in such a way that your *feelings* will be transmitted to the audience. They will feel exactly what you feel. If you feel nothing, they will feel nothing.

10. Work for variety in pitch (highness and lowness of the voice), volume (loudness and softness of the voice), and tempo (slowness and fastness of pace). The reader who uses the same pitch and volume for each phrase will be monotonous, and people will not listen to him.

Resource Books

An Approach to Choral Speech, Mona Swann, St. Martin's Press, New York, N.Y.

Costuming the Biblical Play, Lucy Barton, Baker's Plays, 100 Summer St., Boston, Mass. 02110

Do-It-in-a-Day Puppets, Margaret Weeks Adair, The John Day Company, 62 West 45th St., New York, N.Y.

Play Production, Henning Nelms, Barnes and Noble, Inc., New York, N.Y. (College Outline Series, Paperback)

The Storyteller in Religious Education, Jeanette Perkins Brown, The Pilgrim Press, Boston, Mass.

The Technique of Stage Make-up, Jack Stuart Knapp, Baker's Plays, 100 Summer St., Boston, Mass. 02110

Theatrical Supply Companies

Paramount Theatrical Supplies, 32 W. 20th St., New York, N.Y. 10011, catalog available which lists make-up, gelatin, wigs, lighting equipment, etc.

Max Factor Make-up Studio, Hollywood, California.

INDEX

Candlelight service, 1
Choral speaking, 104
Costumes, 106
Creative reading, 110

Family worship service, 87
Follow spot, 106

Gladden, Washington, 26

"John, the Beloved" (monologue), 100
"Joseph, a Father to the King" (monologue), 13

Lighting, 106
Lord's Supper (instructions for silent Supper), 11

Make-up, 108
Make-up supplies, 112
Missions emphasis, 65
Monologues, 102, 109
　"John, the Beloved," 100
　"Joseph, a Father to the King," 14
　"Saul of Tarsus," 97
　"Woman at the Well," 99

Puppet play, 55
Puppets, making, 62

Resource books, 112

"Saul of Tarsus" (monologue), 97
Scenery, 106
"Shepherd's Story," 26
Slides, how to make, 36
Speech choir, 104
Spotlight, how to improvise, 106
Stories,
　"Shepherd's Story," 26
　"Where Love Is, There God Is Also," 68

Tableaux, arranging, 106
Theatrical supplies, 112
Tolstoi, Leo, 68

"Where Love Is, There God Is Also," 68
"Woman at the Well" (monologue), 99

268.7

McGee, Cecil

Dramatic Programs for Christmas

| 268.7 | | 3717 |
| CLASS | | ACC |

McGee, Cecil
(LAST NAME OF AUTHOR)

Dramatic Programs for Christmas
(BOOK TITLE)

DATE DUE	ISSUED TO
	Jim Willis

X

JEFFERSON AVENUE BAPTIST CHURCH LIBRARY.